The Care and Operation of a Lathe

The purpose of this manual is to enable the beginner to understand the modern metal-cutting lathe, its parts and their functions . . . to teach the proper care of a lathe . . . to explain the grinding of cutters; modern lathe tools and how they should be set-up; methods of holding the work; and, the performance of the basic lathe operations.

While not a "shop kink" book nor a handbook of tables, this manual has the essential "do's and don'ts" and is exceptionally complete in its tool grinding charts.

Published by the
SHELDON MACHINE CO., INC.
CHICAGO, U. S. A.

The Care and Operation of a Lathe

Originally published by
Sheldon Machine Co.
Chicago

Original copyright 1942
by Sheldon Machine Co.

Reprinted by
Lindsay Publications Inc
Bradley IL 60915

ISBN 1-55918-105-2

4 5 6 7 8 9 0

The Care and Operation of a Lathe

The Modern Back Geared Screw Cutting Lathe

From the earliest known lathes in which the work was centered between conveniently spaced trees and revolved with a rope much as a top is spun, years of development have brought the modern back geared screw cutting precision engine lathe—the most perfect and most universal of machine tools. Most perfect, because operating on centers; it is most accurate—most universal, because with its inherent versatility augmented by almost numberless auxiliary attachments, accessories and cutting tools, the modern engine lathe will do almost any machining operation.

Basically, a lathe is a mechanism which will revolve work to be machined against a cutting edge. The modern screw cutting engine lathe is such a mechanism into which has been built (1) means of applying power, (2) strength to cut hard and tough materials, (3) means of holding the cutting point rigidly, (4) means for regulating speed of operation, (5) means for feeding tool into or across, or into and across the work, either manually or by means of "engine" power, under precise control, and (6) means for maintaining a predetermined ratio between rate of revolutions of work and travel of the cutting point or points.

A Primitive Lathe

3

The first screw cutting lathe on record was built in 1740 in France by an unknown machinist, the first American built lathes appeared around 1800. Since that time, thru years of development, of trial and error, certain principles of engine lathe designs have been proven and accepted as standard for all good lathes—differences today being not differences in basic design, parts or operation but primarily in size, capacity, weight, features and refinements; in the quality of materials used and in the excellence of workmanship, accuracy and care in construction.

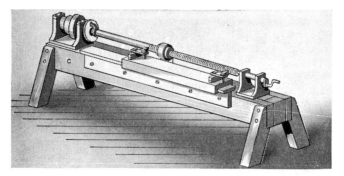

An Early American Screw Cutting Lathe

Because its use is limited only by man's ingenuity, the screw-cutting lathe has played a leading part in American industrial progress as the principal tool used by our experimenters, inventors and mechanics, which does not necessarily mean that the lathe is a tool for geniuses alone. It is a tool which anyone with a fondness for making things can use with both pleasure and profit. Though screw-cutting lathes have become increasingly popular in home shops during the last ten years, there is still the feeling in many minds that the metal cutting lathe is too complex to understand, but actually it is a very reasonable and logical tool that can be mastered by almost anyone.

Risking being elementary, let us start with an understanding of that long name which the metal lathe bears: "back-geared, screw-cutting lathe."

"Back-gear" is a name given to the four gears in the

back of the headstock and quill which provide slow powerful speeds for heavy machining. In other words, the back gears by turning less frequently than the motor or drive wheel give greater leverage or torque at the cutting point — they slow down and increase the power of the lathe spindle which rotates the work being machined.

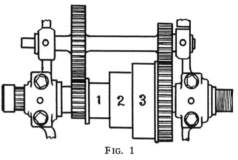

FIG. 1

Fig. 1 illustrates the principle of the back gears—the same principle which may be compared to the multiple pulley hoist. The diagram shows the headstock of a Sheldon lathe with gears uncovered when looked upon from above. The numerals 1, 2 and 3 indicate the three steps of the cone pulley to which the belt is attached for driving the lathe.

Above and to the left of the numeral 1 is the Large Back Gear and above and to the right of numeral 3 is the Small Back Gear, sometimes called the back gear pinion. Directly below the small back gear is the Bull Gear which turns the lathe spindle. When fast spindle speeds are desired for light metal cutting, or for cutting fibre or wood, the Bull Gear Clamp is affixed to the Cone Pulley by letting in the Bull Gear Clamp Push Pin so that the spindle revolves directly with the cone from the belt drive. Such an arrangement is excellent for light work but it does not supply sufficient power for taking heavy cuts in steel and other hard and tough metals. Hence the back gears.

When slow powerful speeds are desired, the bull gear clamp is disengaged by pulling out the push pin so that the 3-stop cone pulley revolves freely on the spindle. Then the back gear lever (No. 11, Fig. 2) is pulled forward enmeshing the large gear with the cone pinion (attached to the 3-step cone pulley) and the small back gear with the bull gear. (Fig. 2) The drive then is

5

from power source to cone, thru cone pinion to large back gear, to gear pinion, to bull gear, to spindle.

This results in a "reduction" in spindle speed which, at the same time, increases the power because the driving member (the cone pulley) makes several revolutions to each one of the driven member (the spindle). Thus it is seen that the back gears are simply a compounding arrangement of gears to increase leverage or power to convert the number of foot pounds put out by the motor into less feet and hence more pounds per foot travelled. They are called back gears because they are located at the back of the headstock.

FIG. 2

Some readers may wonder why slow speeds and variations in speeds of the lathe spindle are necessary. First, slow speeds are needed because metal is being cut by metal and if too high speed is used the tool will burn up. Then some metals like aluminum are soft and may be machined at fast speed without danger or trouble. But hard steels and other metals must be cut at slower speed.

1. 3-Step Cone
2. Cone Gear
3. Large Back Gear
4. Back Gear Pinion
5. Bull Gear
6. Bull Gear Clamp Pull Pin
7. Spindle Nose
8. Reversing Lever (Reverses direction of rotation of lead screw)
9. One of reversing gears
10. Spindle Feed Gear (drives change gears)
11. Back Gear Engagement Lever

The diameter of the work being machined must also be taken into consideration. A point on a 3-in. shaft will actually go past the cutting tool three times as fast as a point on a shaft 1-in. in diameter revolving at the same speed. This is true because that point has to travel a tripled circumference. Thus, for work in any given material the larger the diameter of the work the slower the speeds in spindle revolutions in order to arrive at the desired number of feet per minute cutting speeds.

CHARGE CARD NUMBERS

Expiration Date: _____

☐ Mastercard ☐ Visa

Telephone: (___) _____
Area Code

Signature: _____

SEND COMMENTS and suggestions for Lindsay on a separate piece of paper, so that processing of your order is not slowed down. He reads every note that comes across his desk, but rarely has time to respond. He's too busy finding books, designing catalogs, and a hundred other things!

WE ATTEMPT to keep all books in stock. If a book is out of stock, we'll backorder a copy for you and send it when it arrives. Prices and availability can change at any time.

WHO ELSE SHOULD GET A CATALOG?

If you know someone who would be interested in a copy of this catalog, write his name and address here. We'll see that he gets a copy. A free catalog will be enclosed with your order if you request one.

Lindsay Publications Inc

PO Box 538, Bradley IL 60915-0538 — 815/935-5353

Lindsay Publications Order Form

Customer Number	Name & Address
(from shipping label)	

Date:

_____ Zip Code _____

PRODUCT NO.	TITLE	PRICE

If you run out of room, please use an additional sheet of paper

SUBTOTAL	
Illinois Residents 6 1/4 % sales tax	
TOTAL SENT	

SHIPPING & HANDLING

$1.00 first book
50¢ each additional book for Parcel Post
(Priority Mail, UPS & other types at additional cost)

PO Box 538, Bradley IL 60915-0538 • 815/935-5353 • FAX: 815/935-5477

"Screw-cutting", the other adjective appended to the metal lathe comes from the fact that the lathe is equipped to cut screws or threads in various numbers per inch of material threaded, according to the desire of the operator.

In screw-cutting, which we shall call thread-cutting for clarity, the carriage, which carries the thread-cutting tool, moves by engagement with the rotating lead screw. (Fig. 3) The elementary principle in thread-cutting is that the revolving lead screw pulls the carriage along in the desired direction at a desired speed. The carriage transports the tool rest and the threading tool which cuts the screw-thread into the metal piece being machined.

FIG. 3

Rear View of Sheldon Double Wall Apron showing lead screw. Double Half-nuts for thread cutting and Spline Drive of Power Feeds.

It is evident that the faster the leadscrew revolves in relation to the revolving speed of the spindle the coarser will be the thread as the threading tool will move farther across the revolving metal with each revolution of the work being threaded.

To make this matter more clear, the lathe spindle holding the metal work being screw-cut, revolves at a selected R.P.M. according to the type and size of the work. The lead screw which runs the length of the lathe bed (No. 21, page 10) also revolves at the desired R.P.M., there being a definite and changeable relation or ratio between the spindle speed and the lead screw speed. The manufacturers of lathes have figured this out so that by using various indicated gear combinations the lathe tool automatically cuts the desired number of threads per inch.

In order to operate a lathe it is not essential that the operator fully understand such things as principles of gear ratio and arrangements any more than one needs to understand every detail of design of an automobile

7

in order to operate it successfully. A limited explanation is given for those who like to know the "why" of these things.

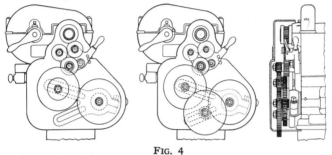

FIG. 4

By changing the gear train between the drive gear and the lead screw gear it is possible to obtain almost any ratio of revolving speed of spindle to revolving speed of lead screw—to obtain any number of threads per inch, or any depth of longitudinal feed. The operation of reversing lever is also illustrated.

A glance at Fig. 4 shows, graphically, how lead screw speeds are changed by means of change gears on a bracket at the headstock end of the lead screw. The sketch is of an independent change gear lathe (a lathe with its complement of "pick-off" gears instead of a lever operated quick change gear box).

All Sheldon lathes except the Metalworker come with semi-quick or full quick change gear boxes which automatically change gear ratios with the shift of a lever. Brass index charts mounted on each Sheldon lathe indicate to the operator the correct pick-off gear com-

FIG. 5

Sheldon Metalworker Lathe
with Pick-off Gears.

Sheldon Lathe with Full
Quick Change Gear Box.

binations to put into the bracket of the Metalworker lathe (or the correct position of the change gear lever on other Sheldon lathes) for cutting any size thread. The gears on the Sheldon Metalworker which are changed are the stud gear and the screw gear, as shown in Fig. 4. Each of the 8 gears supplied with the Sheldon Metalworker (Fig. 5) has the number of its teeth stamped on it so that with the permanent index chart it is easy to select the correct gear combination to give any desired thread pitch. To change the thread pitch (the number of threads per inch) on Sheldon lathes that have a gear box, it is necessary only to place the gear box plunger in the correct indexed hole and the gear-box top lever and the sliding-gear knob in the position indicated on the brass index chart to get any desired thread. (More detailed instructions are given under Thread-cutting in this book.)

Assembly Floor showing production line of Sheldon Lathes with U-Type Underneath Motor Drives.

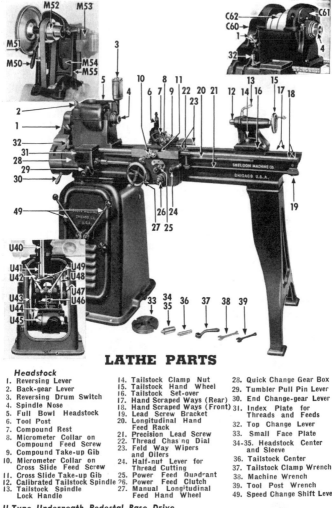

LATHE PARTS

Headstock

1. Reversing Lever
2. Back-gear Lever
3. Reversing Drum Switch
4. Spindle Nose
5. Full Bowl Headstock
6. Tool Post
7. Compound Rest
8. Micrometer Collar on Compound Feed Screw
9. Compound Take-up Gib
10. Micrometer Collar on Cross Slide Feed Screw
11. Cross Slide Take-up Gib
12. Calibrated Tailstock Spindle
13. Tailstock Spindle Lock Handle

14. Tailstock Clamp Nut
15. Tailstock Hand Wheel
16. Tailstock Set-over
17. Hand Scraped Ways (Rear)
18. Hand Scraped Ways (Front)
19. Lead Screw Bracket
20. Longitudinal Hand Feed Rack
21. Precision Lead Screw
22. Thread Chasing Dial
23. Feld Way Wipers and Oilers
24. Half-nut Lever for Thread Cutting
25. Power Feed Quadrant
26. Power Feed Clutch
27. Manual Longitudinal Feed Hand Wheel

28. Quick Change Gear Box
29. Tumbler Pull Pin Lever
30. End Change-gear Lever
31. Index Plate for Threads and Feeds
32. Top Change Lever
33. Small Face Plate
34-35. Headstock Center and Sleeve
36. Tailstock Center
37. Tailstock Clamp Wrench
38. Machine Wrench
39. Tool Post Wrench
49. Speed Change Shift Levers

U-Type Underneath Pedestal Base Drive

U-40. Double V-Belts Spindle Drive

U-41. Spindle Belt Tension Adjustment

U-42. Underneath Drive Countershaft

U-43. Motor V-Belt

U-44. Motor Mounting Plate

U-45. Motor

U-46. Motor Belt Tension Adjustment

U-47. Motor Drive-Shaft and Speed Change Clutches

U-48. Clutch Operated Speed-Change Sheaves & U-Belts

U-49. Speed Change Shift Levers

Headstock Motor Drive

M-50. Belt Tension Release and Adjustment Lever

M-51. V-Belt Motor Sheave

M-52. 3-Step Cone Countershaft

M-53. Motor

M-54. Motor Mounting Plate

M-55. Headstock Motor Drive Mounting Bracket and Housing

Countershaft Drive

C-60. Gear Guards

C-61. Chip Shut-out Door

C-62. 3-Step Cone

The Basic Parts of a Lathe

Those interested in learning the operation of the back-geared, screw cutting lathe are advised to first learn the names and functions of the basic units which make up a lathe. At first glance, the chart may appear complicated to the novice, but with familiarity each part becomes logical and understandable, and with a little practice operation of controls becomes "automatic".

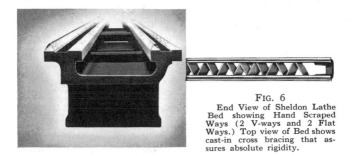

Fig. 6
End View of Sheldon Lathe Bed showing Hand Scraped Ways (2 V-ways and 2 Flat Ways.) Top view of Bed shows cast-in cross bracing that assures absolute rigidity.

1. **Bed.** The bed is the foundation of the lathe, hence must be heavy, strong, should be of one-piece and scientifically braced to assure absolute rigidity. The "Ways" which are found in the top of the bed are the "tracks" upon which carriage and tailstock travels along the bed. In order to maintain an exact relationship between tool point and the work from one end of the lathe to the other, the Ways must be absolutely true and accurate in their alignment to the line of lathe centers and to each other. On quality machine tools the Ways are hand scraped to this accuracy because it is practically impossible to grind accurate V-ways. (The loss of form or diameter resulting from a single pass of a grinding wheel down the length of the bed is sufficient to "throw" the ways "off").

11

2. **Headstock.** The headstock which is secured to the bed, houses the driving mechanism of the lathe—3-step cone, the back gears and the spindle. The spindle which is hollow rotates the work. (Fig. 7)

FIG. 7
The Headstock.

3. **Gears.** Mounted on the "off" left end of the Headstock are the change gears (for thread cutting) and reversing gears for changing the rotational direction of the lathe. (Fig. 4)

4. **Lead Screw.** The lead screw (Fig. 3) runs the length of the bed. Its external thread which is cut with great precision (all Sheldon lead screws are milled on a Pratt and Whitney Special Precision Lead Screw Machine). The lead screw moves the carriage for thread-cutting. It also has a keyway cut its full length with which a spline revolves the worm that moves the lathe carriage when the power feed is engaged (for all purposes but thread-cutting).

5. **The Hand Feed Rack.** Running the length of the bed this rack is geared to the large hand wheel in front of the apron. (No. 20, Page 10) The hand wheel is used for manual transverse feed, and for quick return of the carriageg as when cutting threads, etc.

6. **Tailstock.** The tailstock which provides the right-end support for the work in a lathe can be moved along the lathe bed and anchored at any point on the bed. In the tailstock is the tailstock spindle, the end of which is taper bored to receive the right ("dead") lathe center. The tailstock spindle is actuated in and out by the tailstock hand wheel. (Fig. 8)

FIG. 8
The Tailstock.

7. **Carriage.** The carriage is movable by hand or under power along the bed. It carries the cross slide, com-

pound rest and tool post which hold and maneuver the actual cutting point. (Fig. 9)

8. Apron. Suspended from the front of the carriage is the lathe apron which in turn contains longitudinal feeds (both hand and power), the power feed clutch, power cross feed controls and thread-cutting half nut engagement. The quadrant has 3 positions: (1 top left) engages longitudinal feed; (center position) is "neutral" for hand feed and thread-

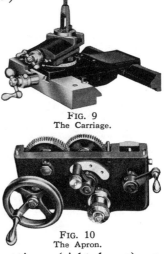

FIG. 9
The Carriage.

FIG. 10
The Apron.

cutting; (right lower) engages power cross feed. Half nut lever is used only for thread-cutting. Sheldon lathes are protected by safety latch which prevents engagement of half nuts and power feeds simultaneously.

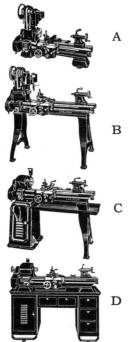

A

B

C

D

9. Legs. All Sheldon lathes are provided with a choice of (A) short bench legs for mounting on a bench or table, (B) floor legs for mounting lathes directly on the floor, or (C) pedestal base which serves both as supporting leg and housing for underneath motor drives. (D) Metal (or Wood Bench) with Underneath Motor Drive and tool and equipment storage drawers.

13

Micrometer Control and Calibration

You will note that just inside the ball crank handles of both the cross feed and the compound rest feed there are calibrated collars. (Fig. 11) These micrometer dial collars (each calibration represents one thousandth of an inch) can be moved independently around the

FIG. 11
Shows micrometer collars on Cross Feed, and Compound Feed Screw. "A" points to Tool Post, "B" shows how loose internal gibb collar prevents pitting of shaft of Sheldon Feed Screw.

shaft of the feed screw or locked to it with a small thumb screw. The collars can be thus zeroed at any point and the depth of feed from that point read on the dial. In use, if you desire to reduce a diameter being machined a known number of thousandths of an inch there need be no guess work about it, for by setting the collar at zero you can then, by watching the movement of the dial, know the depth of the feed from the zeroing point — each calibrated line on the collar that passes the zero mark means the tool has been advanced into the work .001 of an inch.

NOTE: To reduce a diameter a given number of thousandths of an inch the tool is advanced but one-half as many thousandths on the dial. This is because, cutting a continuous chip completely around the work, the tool cuts an equal amount from BOTH sides. Example: To reduce the diameter of a shaft .005 inch you would only advance the tool .0025 (Fig. 11) (2½ calibrations) as this will cut .0025 off from each side and .0025 inch + .0025 inch = .005 inch taken off the diameter of the shaft.

NOTE: Before zeroing be sure that the tool has engaged the work before setting the collar as every screw to be movable must have some play in the thread. Likewise when backing the cutting tool away from the cut it is necessary to move the feed screw sufficiently to first take up the "back lash" or lost motion in the screw before "setting" the collar or when drawing the tool from cut, to remember that until this slight "play" is taken up the tool will not start moving.

To assure permanent accuracy of setting of micrometer collars on Sheldon lathes, the thumb set screw bears on an inner floating collar which serves as a gib and prevents the pitting of the feed screw shaft. As zeroing can be at any point, the slightest pit in the shaft would tend to draw the adjustment screw point thus destroying the accuracy of the zeroing. (B, Fig. 11)

FIG. 12   FIG. 13

Calibrations on the base of the compound rest are carried completely around the base (360°) and numbered in degrees from 90° right to 90° left. (Fig. 12)

Calibrations on the Tailstock Ram are in sixteenths of an inch (Fig. 13) as are the calibrations for tailstock set-over.

Drives. Power is supplied to the lathes either thru countershafts with a step down cone that inversely matches the cone in the lathe headstock and which is driven from line shafting by an individual motor, or by means of an integral or attached individual motor drive.

Countershafts are of 3 types (Fig. 14): Simple countershafts for (1) flat belt line shaft drive (2) for "V"-belt motor drive, and (3) Double friction countershafts which provide means for instantly reversing the direction of lathe rotation.

The countershaft is usually mounted above the lathe but can also be mounted behind the lathe (as on the back wall or even on the floor) though a back drive is theoretically, if not actually inefficient.

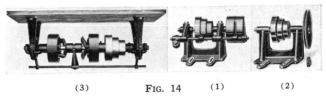

(3)   FIG. 14   (1)   (2)

15

Motor Drives. The trend in modern shop layout is to individual short center motor drives as a means of eliminating overhead belt and shafting and saving power. All Sheldon lathes have a number of optional motor drives including: **Overhead Motor Drive.**

FIG. 15

Mounts on the headstock replacing the top half of the bowl, providing a ¾ bowl head motor mounting, instant belt release for cone belt and individual tension adjustments for both motor and cone belts. It contains a 3-stage flat belt or 4-stage V-belt cone which operates in either needle or precision ball bearings. It is an exceedingly efficient (up pull), convenient and space saving drive. (Fig. 15)

FIG. 16

The Sheldon Underneath Motor Drive for enclosure in pedestal base leg or in a cabinet bench, come in two types, one lever operated thru clutches, the other with double cones. Both are 4-speed V-belt drives and both permit the use of standard 1-piece lathe beds, and full bowl (completely housed) headstocks. These are the finest drives yet developed for moderate sized lathes. (Fig. 16)

The Sheldon Back Motor Drives are provided for the Sheldon Metalworker (home work shop) lathes in both bench and floor types. While excellent back drives, these are not recommended for heavy duty industrial use because back drives are not as effi-

FIG. 17

cient as either overhead or underneath drives and increase floor space requirements. (Fig. 17)

The Theory
of Metal Cutting

Since no machine tool can in the final analysis be more efficient than its cutting edge, and since in the operation of a lathe the operator must continuously re-grind and re-sharpen the cutting tools, it is well for every operator to know something of the theory of metal cutting . . . to know how a cutting edge cuts metal, how metal cutting tool shapes are determined and why they differ so radically from the knives and other wood cutting tools.

All cutting with a sharp edge, whether it be with a thin blade of a slicing knife or the almost square edge of a closely supported carbide tool, is basically a wedging-apart action. Obviously, the first essential to any wedging tool is a penetrating edge. It is also obvious that the narrower the blade the less force or power will be required to "wedge" it thru the material to be cut. Therefore, when cutting comparatively soft materials with a cutting tool fashioned from much harder and stronger substance, the blade can be very thin and can be sharpened to a long thin edge. As the hardness (or resistance to separation) of the material to be cut increases, the *strength* of cutting edge must also be increased. A knife sharpened to too thin an edge quickly dulls, even when cutting wood or other comparatively soft material. Try to cut a nail or even softer metals with even a fine steel blade and it loses its keenness instantly, though the steel in the blade is harder than the metal cut. Examine the edge under a glass and you discover why —the edge has been bent or broken off. This introduces an additional factor, the *strength* of the cutting edge which explains

FIG. 18

17

why the knife edge breaks off almost upon contact with metal while the more obtuse cutting-edge of a cold chisel will stand up to continuous pounding into metal. (Fig. 18)

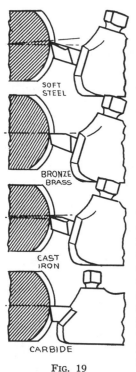

SOFT STEEL

BRONZE BRASS

CAST IRON

CARBIDE

FIG. 19

Then let us put it down as primary that the cutting edge of any metal-cutting tool must first be *strong* and hence closely supported. This is more easily understood when we realize the tremendous force (on a lathe downward pressure) exerted against the cutting-edge — pressure against cutting tools as great as 250,000 per sq. in. have been measured on large metal cutting lathes.

The cutting action of a lathe is as follows: With the work revolving, a strong, rigidly held cutting edge is forced under the surface of the work. As the work is revolved against (pressed down against) the cutting edge small bits (chips) or a continuous ribbon of metal is wedged away from the material being machined (Fig. 20). Only in soft ductile materials is this wedging action continuous. On harder substances the wedging force compresses, rises to the shearing point and shears . . . builds up, shears again, etc., repeatedly. This is shown in the distortion of chips when cuts are heavy and materials hard. (Fig. 20)

When the vibration of shearing synchronizes with the natural vibration period of any part of the tool, tool holder or work it is called "chatter". Hence the way to eliminate "chatter" is to change one of the harmonizing factors—by making the tool more rigid, holding the cutter closer-up in the tool holder, backing the tool holder farther into the tool post, or altering the feed of the tool, the operating speed of the lathe, or the angle of cutter bit to the work.

Long years of experience have established certain principles of tool design and tool approach, and various tool and cutting angles as the most efficient for various operations. These factors of tool design, cutting angles and tool approach are now largely taken care of in the design of the tool holders and need be considered by the lathe operator only insofar as they effect the grinding of the cutters used. For example, the standard turning tool designed for high speed steel cutters holds cutters at an angle of 14½° above horizontal. Hence, in this position the tool needs to be "backed-off" from the cutting edge 14½° more in order to clear the work than would be required if the tool were held in an exactly horizontal position. (Fig. 19) However, when machining with a carbide tipped tool, because of the brittleness of the cutting edge the cutter is fed to the work horizontally on dead center—a position requiring an absolute minimum of back grinding and permitting close-up support of the cutting edge.

Sharpness of the Tool Edge

Sharpness or keenness of the cutting edge instead of being the all-important factor in determining tool performance as it is with a pocket or kitchen knife is just one of many performance factors on metal cutting tools. On rough or heavy cuts it is far less important than strength for a false cutting edge or crust usually builds up on the tool edge and though it "dulls" the angle of the edge often increases its efficiency by increasing its wedging action. (Fig. 20) Shapes of cutters are usually more important than edges which are generally rough ground and usu-

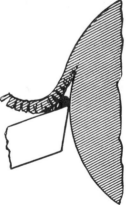

FIG. 20

Illustrates Wedging-off action of Metal-cutting tool, cutting hard steel. Black portion illustrates the false edge or crust which often builds up on cutting edge.

ally need to be honed only for very fine finishing cuts or for work in soft and ductile materials like brass or aluminum. Lack of clearances that would permit a tool to drag on the work below the cutting edge would act as a brake on the lathe and greatly reduce pressure on the cutting point and thus would interfere more with tool performance than the dullness of the edge itself. At the same time excessive clearance makes a tool weak, means lack of support to the cutting-edge. Such an edge is certain to break-off if used on hard materials.

Clearance requirements change with almost every operation and are multiplex for all in that clearance must be provided not only from the cutting edge; there must be end clearance, side clearance and, in order to help the chip to pass with minimum resistance across the top of the tool, it often should have top rake as well. The determining of proper shapes and rakes to which tools should be ground has already been done for us by such specialized organizations as the Armstrong Bros. Tool Co., of Chicago who have developed the "Armstrong System of Tool Holders" that are now "used in over 96% of the machine shops and tool rooms." Grinding charts as worked out by "The Tool Holder People" are given at the end of this chapter. (See Pages 26-38)

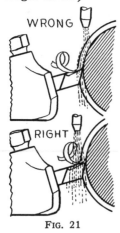

WRONG

RIGHT

Fig. 21

Heat a Bi-product of Metal Cutting

The energy expended at the cutting point of a lathe is largely converted into heat, and because the energy expended is great the heat generated is intense. Before the development of today's High Speed Steel this heat created the most serious machining problem because machining could only be done under a steady flow of coolant which was needed to prevent the tool from heating up to its annealing point, softening and breaking down.

Advancement in metallurgy lead to the development of high speed steel — steels alloyed with Tungsten, that instead of annealing becomes harder at cutting temperatures. Today with high speed steel, cutting is largely "dry"—coolants are seldom used on small lathes except when they are run at extremely high speeds on continuous heavy-duty production work. While high speed steels are self-hardening even when red hot (950F) they do not dissipate the heat, nor in any way prevent the work from heating up, often faster than its revolving can cool it. Since steels expand when heated it is well, especially when working on long shafts, to constantly check the tightness of the lathe centers to be sure that the expansion of the work does not cause centers to bind. In certain everyday lathe operations however (thread-cutting or knurling for example) the use of a cutting-oil or other *lubricant* is always recommended. On such work, especially if the cut is light and the lathe speed slow, a brush occasionally dipped in oil and held against the work will provide sufficient lubrication. (Fig. 22) However, for continuous high-speed heavy-duty production work, especially on tough alloy steels the use of cutting-oil or a coolant will increase cutting efficiency and is essential if other than high speed cutting tools are used. All types of Sheldon lathes are available equipped with complete lubricating or coolant re-circulating systems. When a coolant is used it should be directed against the cutting point and cutter as in Fig. 21.

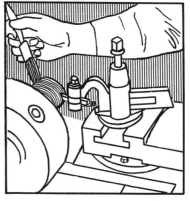

FIG. 22

Holding brush dipped in cutting oil on work as for thread-cutting or knurling.

Cutting speeds generally employed have been carried over from the old "forged tool" days and are:

```
Cast iron............from 40 to 90 feet per minute
Steel...............from 35 to 150 feet per minute
Brass..............from 150 to 200 feet per minute
Aluminum.............200 or more feet per minute
Monel Metal...........120 or more feet per minute
Stainless Steel..........40 or more feet per minute
Plastics* ...................2 to 30 feet per minute
*Ample use of cutting oil recommended
```

With modern lathes and modern tool holders equipped with high speed steel cutters, far higher cutting speeds than the customary speeds listed above are possible without loss of efficiency. After you have become well acquainted with your Sheldon lathe and have the "feel" of the tool you will be able to test out these higher cutting speeds in order to better understand the productive capacity of your lathe. The custom of increasing speeds and feeds up to a vibration or "chatter" point and then taking an operating speed just below that point is not a true measure of a machine tool's capacity for it is frequently the case that if speed is increased beyond this critical vibration speed, a wide range of faster, smooth-cutting speeds will be found above the first "chatter" speed.

The Armstrong Tool Holder System

In the old days every machine shop had to have its blacksmith or "tool dresser" to forge, heat treat and grind tools for every operation on each machine tool and when dulled to re-form, re-harden and re-grind them while men and machines stood idle. A half century ago the "Armstrong principle" of tool design was introduced — the principle of permanent multi-purpose drop forged shanks or tool holders which held inserted cut-

Straight Holder Tool

L. H. Off-Set Tool Holder

R. H. Off-Set Tool Holder

ters anyone could grind from standard high speed steel shapes. Today the use of tool holders for all standard lathe operations has become universal, and tool forging is now largely confined to making of special form tools. With 7 or 8 tool holders and a selection of interchangeable cutter bits the operator is permanently tooled-up for every lathe operation because each tool holder with its complement of cutters will do the work of a complete set of forged tools. (See page 24) Problems of tool design, tool strength, tool approach, tool clearance and cutting angles have all been worked out in testing laboratories and the shops of the world and are built into the tool holder. Today every man grinds his own cutters and is his own "tool dresser".

Carbide Tool Holder

Straight Side Tool

Spring Cutting-off Tool

R. H. Off-Set Cutting-off

Boring Tool

3-Bar Boring Tool

Spring Threading Tool

Threading Tool

Knurling Tool

Grinding Cutter Bits
for Lathe Tools

High Speed Tool Bits for use in Tool Holders

Square

While modern tool holders take tool bits or cutters any mechanic can quickly grind from stock shapes of high speed steel, namely from "squares", "flats" and "bevels", many of the shops buy their cutters either "ready-ground" (as illustrated below), or as "ready-to-grind" bits or blades (as above and in Fig. 23). Ready-ground and ready-to-grind bits and blades are sold by brand names are of specially selected high speed steel, cut to length and properly heat treated. They are fine tools in the rough and are generally superior to high speed steel shapes sold by the pound.

Bevel

Special
Shape for
Side Tools

24

Standard Cutter Forms

Ready Ground High Speed Steel cutters are provided in the 10 standard cutter forms illustrated below.

1 Left Hand Turning Tool	2 Round Nose Turning Tool	3 Right Hand Turning Tool	4 Left Hand Corner Tool	5 Threading Tool

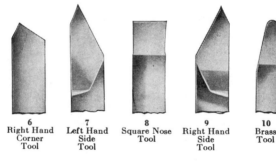

6 Right Hand Corner Tool	7 Left Hand Side Tool	8 Square Nose Tool	9 Right Hand Side Tool	10 Brass Tool

*For application of these cutter
forms in test holders, see page 68*

High Speed Steel Blades

Special High Speed Steel Blades (Fig. 23) as differ-
ated "Bits" are also carried by all tool sellers "ready-
ground" or "ready-to-gind". These Blades are of two
cross sectional shapes — the "bevel" used in cutting-
off tool holders and the
"special" designed for
side tool holders.

FIG. 23

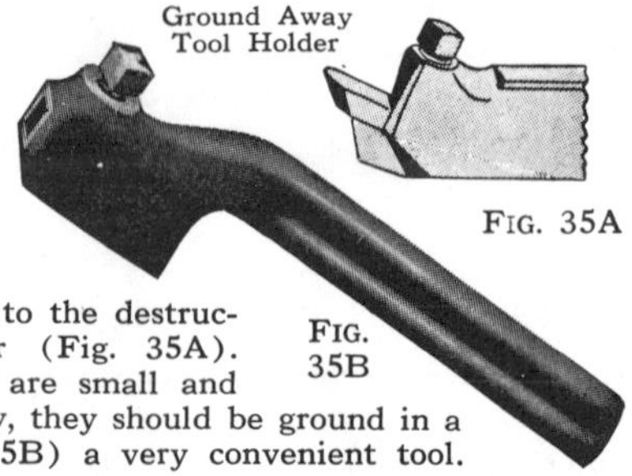

Use of Grinding Holders. The practice of grinding or "touching up" cutters while they are in the tool holder is exceedingly risky and is not permitted in properly operated shops because it eventually leads to the destruction of the tool holder (Fig. 35A). Especially where cutters are small and difficult to hold accurately, they should be ground in a Grinding Holder (Fig. 35B) a very convenient tool.

Ground Away Tool Holder

FIG. 35A

FIG. 35B

Grinding Cutter Bits for Lathe Tools

In grinding High Speed Steel cutter bits there are five purposes to be kept in mind (1st) to provide a strong, keen, cutting edge or point—*angle of keenness;* (2nd) to provide the proper cutting form—*the correct or most convenient shape for a specific operation;* (3rd) to provide clearance away from the point of the tool—*front clearance;* (4th) to provide clearance away from the side of the tool — *side rake;* (5th) to provide free chip movement over the tool and away from the cutting edge. Angles of "keenness" can vary from 60° for mild softness to 90° for hard steels and castings. (Fig. 24) Front clearance must always be sufficient to clear

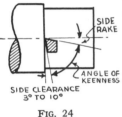

SIDE RAKE
ANGLE OF KEENNESS
SIDE CLEARANCE
3° TO 10°

FIG. 24

the work but if too great will weaken the edge and cause it to break off. (Fig. 25) Side rake and back rake requirements vary with the material used, and the operation to be performed. So many factors enter in determining exact shapes and rakes for cutter-bits, so many theories have

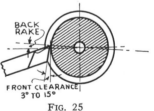

BACK RAKE
FRONT CLEARANCE
3° TO 15°

FIG. 25

been "proven" and again "disproven" regarding every phase of this subject that for practical purposes the safest procedure is to adopt the shapes and rakes developed thru years of research by the manufacturers of Armstrong Tool Holders which have been generally adopted, and are reproduced on the following pages.

26

Grinding High Speed Steel Cutters

Cutters should be ground on a true surfaced good quality medium grit grinding wheel (preferably an 8 inch, 46A grit to 60 grit or 68A grit carborundum wheel, operating at 6000 rpm or 6500 rpm.) When starting with an unground cutter bit the procedure is

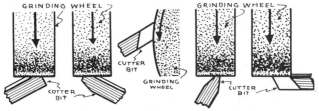

Fig. 26

usually to (1st) grind the left side clearance, (2nd) grind the right side clearance (3rd) grind the end Form or Radius (4th) grind the End Clearance and (5th) grind the Top Rake touching in a chip crater, if any, last. (Figs. 26, 31) If honing the cutting edge (for fine finishing cut or machining soft materials) it should be done by drawing the cutter away from the cutting edge across the oil stone. (Fig. 27)

Fig. 27

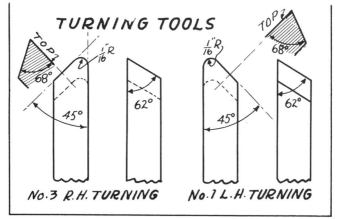

No.3 R.H. TURNING   No.1 L.H. TURNING

27

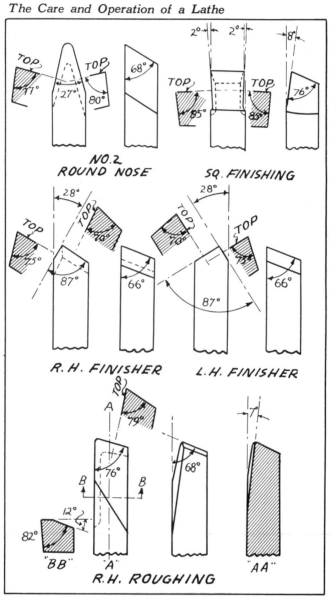

Turning Tools

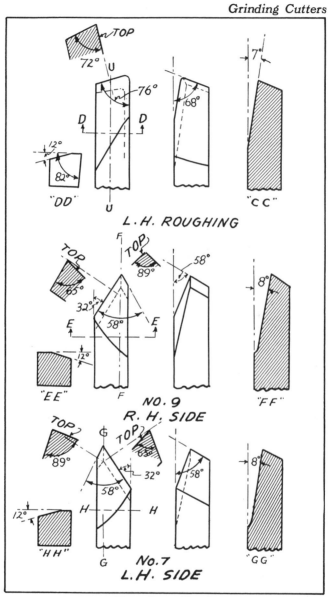

TOP

72° U

76°

68°

7°

D   D

12°

82°

"DD"

U

"CC"

L.H. ROUGHING

F

TOP   TOP

65°   89°   58°

32°

58°   E

E   8°

12°

"EE"

F   "FF"

NO. 9
R.H. SIDE

TOP   TOP

89°   68°

32°   58°

58°

12°   H   H

58°   8°

"HH"

G   "GG"

No.7
L.H. SIDE

Turning Tools

29

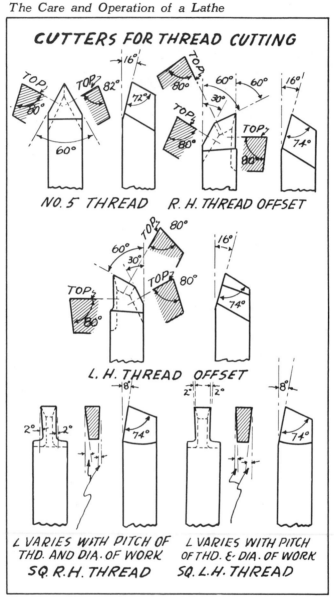

Threading Tools

Grinding Cutters for Boring and Cutting Internal Threads

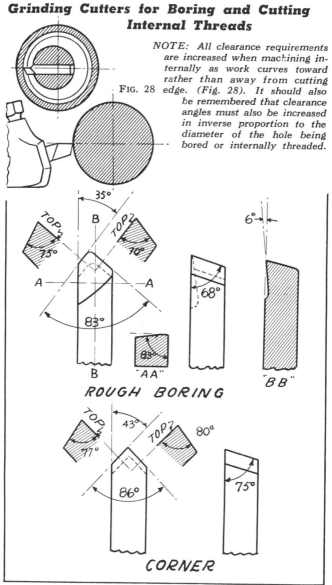

NOTE: All clearance requirements are increased when machining internally as work curves toward rather than away from cutting edge. (Fig. 28). It should also be remembered that clearance angles must also be increased in inverse proportion to the diameter of the hole being bored or internally threaded.

FIG. 28

ROUGH BORING

CORNER

Boring Tools

31

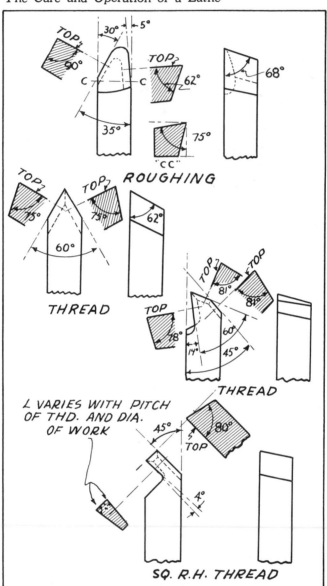

ROUGHING

THREAD

THREAD

∠ VARIES WITH PITCH
OF THD. AND DIA.
OF WORK

SQ. R.H. THREAD

Internal Tools

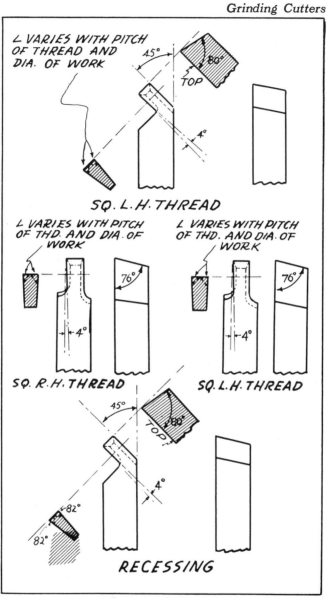

Internal Tools

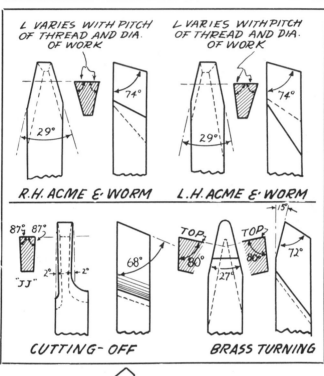

L VARIES WITH PITCH OF THREAD AND DIA. OF WORK

R.H. ACME & WORM

74°
29°

L VARIES WITH PITCH OF THREAD AND DIA. OF WORK

L.H. ACME & WORM

74°
29°

CUTTING-OFF

87¾° 87°
"JJ"
2° 2°
68°

BRASS TURNING

TOP
80°
15°
72°
TOP
80°
27°

FIG. 1

FIG. 2

FIG. 3

CUTTER GRINDING GAUGE

For schools, as an aid to beginners, and in industrial work where long production runs require periodic re-grinding to identical rakes, a Cutter Grinding Gauge (as illustrated) simplifies grinding and provides means for a quick check of Tool Angle (Fig. 1), End Rake (Fig. 2) and Side Rake (Fig. 3).

Special Grindings for Machining Materials other than Steel

Because as pointed out at the beginning of this chapter when grinding high speed steel cutters, cutting *angles* are determined primarily by requirements of strength rather than requirements of keenness. Angles and rakes given on the preceeding cutter grinding charts have been established for general industrial tool room and machine shop use. In machining steel it can be safely accepted as a general rule that the

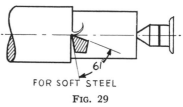

FOR SOFT STEEL

FIG. 29

softer the steel, the keener the angle of the cutting edge—for soft steels to angles as acute as 61°. (Fig. 29)

The same general rule applies to cast iron. While chilled cast iron or very hard grades of cast iron re-

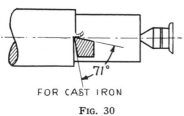

FOR CAST IRON

FIG. 30

quire tools with cutting edge angles as great as 85°, for ordinary cast iron, the greatest efficiency is obtained with a more acute cutting edge as of approximately 71°. (Fig. 30).

Grinding Bits for Turning and Machining Brass

Brasses have a tendency to pull or "drag" when being machined and because of the characteristics peculiar to brasses they are best machined on dead center with top rake in the horizontal plane of the lathe centers. Brass being softer than steel requires less support for the cutting edge, but requiring an almost flat top angle brass cutters can gain greater angle of keenness only in increased side and end rakes (See grinding instruction on round nose brass cutter preceeding grinding

The Care and Operation of a Lathe

charts). It is often advisable to hone cutting edges of cutters to be used for machining brass.

NOTE: All round nose cutters are ground with flat tops and with equal side rakes because they are fed across the work both to the right and to left.

Grinding Special Chip Guides

When cutting-off blades especially, and occasionally on other cutter bits where because of extreme hardness or toughness of material being machined there is difficulty in controlling the chip leaving the work, it is sometimes helpful to grind a smooth round crater just behind the cutting edge which will serve as a chip guide and start the chip curling smoothly. (Fig. 31)

Fig. 31

Using a Center Gauge for Checking "V" Thread Form

While the use of factory made Form Cutters for thread cutting has become general practice, there are occasions when it is convenient to grind a standard cutter bit for such use, especially for cutting standard 60 degree V-threads. In grinding an ordinary square cutter to make a thread-cutting tool great care should be taken to insure a true thread form. This is most

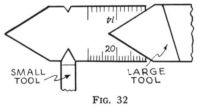

SMALL TOOL

LARGE TOOL

Fig. 32

easily done by using an ordinary center gauge if grinding a standard V-thread tool or a special thread gauge for any of the special thread forms.

Grinding an Ordinary 60° V-Threading Tool

To grind a cutter for an ordinary V-thread; grind the left side of the tool to 30° then the right side at 30°, being careful to grind equally from both sides so that the point of the tool will be centered. Then test for true form by inserting newly ground point in closest

36

sized "V" in a standard center gauge (Fig. 32) holding gauge and cutter up to the light. When ground perfectly no light streak will show between the tool and the gauge. Other rakes should be taken from grinding chart.

Grinding a Tool Bit for ACME or other Special Threads

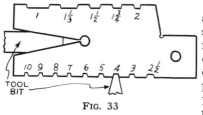

FIG. 33

Thread gauges are available for all standard threads. Before grinding such cutters be sure to ascertain the correct pitch angle of the particular thread profile. For example you will note the pitch of an **ACME** Thread is 29° to a side and that the point of the tool is ground back square to an exact thread profile that requires a different end width for each thread size. Because it is essential that thread forms be accurate if threads are to fit snugly and smoothly, and because every re-sharpening of this type of cutter requires the regrinding of the entire form, it is far better practice where any amount of threading is to be done to use a special threading tool that takes a special form cutter. Such cutters require only flat, top grinding (which does not alter the cutting profile), to sharpen. They are described under "Thread-Cutting" later in this book. (Page 86)

"Carbide" Tip Cutters and Cutter Forms

New "Carbide" cutting materials have been developed that approach the diamond in hardness. While these new "carbides" permit the easy machining of chilled cast iron, hard and tough steels, hard rubber, bakelite, glass and other difficult or "unmachinable" materials, the primary use of carbide in the metalworking industries is for long production runs on ordinary steels. On such work (quantity production work) carbide tipped tools permit higher running speeds *and much longer runs between re-grindings.* The cutting edge of carbide tools will stand up from 10 to 200 times as long as the edge of high speed steel tools.

Cutting Carbides are of two main types, namely Tungsten-carbides and Tantalum-carbides. Both are sintered materials—are composed of minute carbide crystals held together by a binder, (like the grains of a grind stone, hence the prefix *Cemented* Tungsten Carbide etc. All carbides are extremely expensive and

FIG. 34

being extremely hard are extremely brittle and susceptible to fractures from shock, hence solid carbide cutters are impractical and all carbide tools and cutters are really alloy steel tools and cutters with a small piece of carbide inserted at the cutting point. (Fig. 34)

While valuable for special applications, for long production runs the machining of hardened parts without annealing (as in maintenance and repair work) and the machining of exceedingly hard and tough alloy steels or "dragging" materials like bakelite or hard rubber, the general use of carbide cutter for general work in the tool room or machine shop is not recommended because (1st) they are extremely expensive, and (2nd) their safe handling requires the development of a special technique—a new "feel" for feeding these tools.

If however, you have occasion to use carbide cutters for the first time, *feed the cutter to the work very slowly.* Above all avoid abrupt contacts and shock to the tool point for compared with steel all "carbides" are exceedingly brittle.

Uncrating and
Setting Up a Sheldon Lathe

All Sheldon Lathes come completely assembled, tightened up and ready to be placed on the floor, oiled and put to work. They come crated with bench legs, floor legs or pedestal base and motor drives (if any) attached, with all machined and hand scraped parts protected with heavy grease, all unmachined parts painted, the entire lathe wrapped in a water and grease-proof cover and strongly braced and crated. In each crate is a box of "Standard Equipment".

When uncrating, first remove inside cross braces, then remove bottom outside cross braces, loosen upright boards completely around the base and lift the crate off the lathe. Great care should be taken in loosening crate as a slip of the hammer or bar can do serious damage to the lathe.

FIG. 35—Sheldon Bench Lathe crated for local delivery. In uncrating first loosen all cross braces and uprights at bottom and lift crate off the lathe.

39

With lathe uncrated, next open your box of "Standard Equipment" and check items included against the "Standard Equipment" listed with that model lathe in the Sheldon Catalog. After all parts are accounted for, crating materials may be removed and you are ready to move your lathe into working position.

In selecting the proper location for your lathe remember that (1) operation is from the apron side of lathe, allow at least 40″ to 48″ operator clearance in front of the lathe. (2) That the best working light should shine over the operator's

FIG. 36

shoulder and should be ample. (3) That lathe must be on a solid (concrete if possible) foundation. If on wood floor—flooring should be braced, if necessary, to prevent sagging or settling, because the lathe must be set solidly, squarely and rigidly on bed and must be *level* if it is to work accurately. (4) That allowance should be made at back, end and above for later addition of taper attachments, overhead motor drive or other accessories. End clearance off the headstock should be provided where possible if bar stock is to be fed thru the spindle. Where the placing of more than one lathe is contemplated arrangement in oblique rows will save much floor space as long bar stock for each machine can be fed from stock rests placed behind the adjacent lathe. (5) Bench lathes should be mounted on a *heavy, rigid and level* bench which should be about 28″ high.

Before permanently anchoring the lathe to the floor or bench be sure that the bed is absolutely level. *Remember, no lathe can do accurate work unless it is solidly anchored and level.* Use an accurate level, both along and across the bed. Shim up any low points in floor or bench using sheet metal or other non-compressable material. After tightening anchor bolts, check again for level. (Fig. 36)

Hanging the Countershaft

When operating the lathe from vertical line shafting another factor must be considered in determining the location of the lathe—the axis of the lathe cone and countershaft cones must be parallel while their relationship to the line shaft must be such that the pull is uniform across the belt and cones. This is most easily done where space permits by having all axies parallel i.e. cone to countershaft to lineshaft. (Fig. 37)

Calculating the speed of Pulleys

The speed of any pulley can be easily computed by starting with the rated speed (R.P.M.) of the prime mover. By multiplying its number of revolutions indicated on motor plate, by the circumference of the motor pulley, one gets the number of feet per minute travelled by the primary drive belt. By dividing the "number of feet per minute" travelled by the driven pulley (which will be the same as that of the driving motor pulley, ignoring slippage) *by* the circumference of the driven pulley one will have the R.P.M. of the line shaft, and by the same procedure can compute the speed of the countershaft, etc.

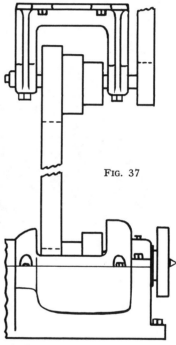

FIG. 37

Oiling the Lathe

Set-up and hooked-up, the lathe is ready for oiling. *This must be done carefully and thoroughly* before starting the lathe. To this end provide yourself with a *pressure oil can* and a supply of good quality *SAE No. 20 Machine oil*.

In order that the oiling may be thorough and complete we suggest that you follow the oiling routine given here step by step.

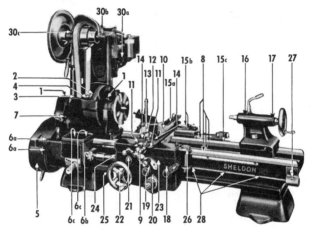

Oiling the Headstock

(If the lathe has an underneath motor drive with full bowl headstock, first remove top cover casting so that cone and back gears are exposed.)

1. Fill the two oil cups above the spindle bearings.

2. Turn back gears until oil button in middle of back gear shaft is exposed then with pressure oil can, pump enclosed oil reservoir full of oil thru this button.

3. Squirt a few "shots" of oil into the thrust bearing (just inside the left spindle bearing).

4. Turn 3-step cone around until socket set screw is exposed —remove set screw and pump considerable oil inside cone, then replace the set screw.

4a. If the lathe has an underneath motor drive you will find the oil button on cone directly to the left of the large spindle gear.

5. Swing out gear guard so that pick-off gears are exposed. All idler (and pick-off) gears have an oil hole drilled in the hub. Oil each of these. Then put a few drops of oil on the teeth of all gears.

6. If the lathe has a Quick-Change Gear Box:
   (6a) Fill the two oil cups on the left side of the change gear housing.
   (6b) Fill the two oil cups on the right side of the change gear housing.
   (6c) Remove cover of change gear and fill the 4 oil holes found at the hubs of the shifting gears and long compound gear.

7. Pull down the Reversing Lever and you will find the next oil cup just above it.

Oiling the Ways

8. Next run the carriage as far to the left as possible, put a few drops of oil on the V-ways and Flat-ways. Run the carriage to the extreme right and repeat.

Oiling the Carriage

9. Directly inside the micrometer indexing collar of the cross feed you will find an oil button. Force oil in there.

10. Put a few drops of oil on the cross feed worm.

11. Put a few drops of oil along the cross feed ways.

12. You will find another oil button inside the micrometer indexing collar of the compound. Put oil in there.

13. Put a few drops of oil on the Compound Feed Screw.
14. Put a few drops of oil on Compound Slides.
15. If the lathe comes with a Taper Attachment:
    (15a) You will find an oil button on the taper attachment saddle just in front of the locking handle. Fill this reservoir with your pressure can.
    (15b) Put a few drops of oil on the swivel.
    (15c) Loosen the 2 binding screws that hold the taper attachment bracket to the rear flat way so that this bracket will slide freely with the movement of the carriage when not taper turning. Put a few drops of oil on the rear flat-way on either side of the bracket and move carriage and hence the bracket back and forth along the way with the longitudinal hand feed wheel.

Oiling the Tailstock

16. Directly on top at the left end of the Tailstock you will find an oil button. This will take considerable oil as it feeds the tailstock spindle reservoir.
17. There is an oil hole near the Tailstock Hand Wheel; oil the hand wheel bearing and screw there.

Oiling the Apron

18. There is an oil button at the top of the boss for the half-nuts (thread cutting) engagement lever.

19. An oil button directly on the boss where the longitudinal and Cross Feed Quadrant Lever enters the apron.
20. Another oil button is found on the top of the Clutch Engagement Hand Screw.
21. At the top left corner the oil button provides means for oiling the Tranverse Rack Pinion Gear Stud.
22. Another oil button is found at the Hub of the Longitudinal Feed Hand Wheel.
23. Above the "cross feed" position of the Quadrant Lever is an oil duct hole—put in plenty here as this duct oils the worm feed, spline and lead screw.
24. On the left end of the apron at top you will find an oil cup —this is where you oil the Quadrant and Gears of the Apron.
25. Also below the No. 24 oil cup is an oil duct hole where oil is supplied into the apron sump for the internal splash lubricating system.

NOTE: Below and to the left of the Clutch Hand Screw is a horizontal oil cup fitting. This is not an oiling point but rather an oil overflow point which maintains oil level in the apron sump at a constant level.

Oiling the Thread Chasing Dial

26. There is an oil hole at the top of the Thread Chasing Dial housing.

Oiling the Lead Screw

27. There is an oil button in the front center of the bracket which supports the right end of the lead screw.
28. Put a few drops of oil along the lead screw.

Oiling the Motor Drive

30. Lathe illustrated has Sheldon Overhead Motor Drive, so we have included: See that (30a) Motor Oil cups are full and fill the oil reservoirs at either end of the 3-step cone countershaft — thru the two oil cups (30b - 30c) found over shaft bearings.

Automatic Lubrication of High Speed Lathe Spindle Bearings

On Sheldon High Speed Lathes — those with spindle speeds higher than 1200 R.P.M., self lubricating hand scraped high speed semi-steel cast bearings, super-precision pre-loaded ball bearing or ultra-precision roller bearings are used since bronze bearings cannot stand up to such speeds.

When cast iron bearings are used they are made self-lubricating by an automatic oil circulating system consisting of a reservoir of oil, a felt wick supported by a spring, and feeder groove and overflow return grooves around the outside of the bearings. In operation the centrifugal force generator by the high speed spindle carries oil up to the juncture of 2-piece bearing covers and superfluous oil overflowing between section is returned to the reservoir by way of the return grooves.

(Top)
Spindle with Bronze Bearing
(Center)
Spindle with Ball Bearing
(Bottom)
Spindle with Roller Bearing

NOTE: Ball or roller headstock bearings and ball thrust bearings in draw in collet attachment should be oiled with a good grade of machine oil every time the lathe is used.

"Running-in" the Lathe

Though all Sheldon Lathes are "run-in" at the factory, it is always well to put them thru an additional short breaking-in run before putting them to work. After the lathe is completely oiled check the belts of counter shaft or motor drive to be sure tension is correctly adjusted (means are provided for adjusting individually the tension of all belts on Sheldon lathes) to see that all belts are at correct tension. Then:

1. Loosen binding screw at top of Thread Chasing Dial and swing actuating gear out of engagement with lead screw and re-tighten screw. To keep the thread dial indicator in constant engagement (except when cutting threads) causes unnecessary wear on lead screw.

2. Put the Power Feed Quadrant on the apron in the neutral position so that neither longitudinal nor power cross feeds are engaged.

3. **Disengage the back gears.** (See Fig. 2) First, disengage the back gears by (a) throwing the back-gear lever back (No. 11), (b) turn the cone until the engaging pin is over the engaging hole in the face gear. Let the pin of the Bull Gear Clamp Pull Pin (No. 6) into the hole on the face gear.

4. **Start the Motor** and let the lathe run for 15 minutes on its direct drive.

5. If the spindle bearings are running cool and everything seems to be working smoothly it's time to try the lathe with back gears. WARNING: Never engage the back gear while the lathe is running. The inertia built up by the high velocity of a direct drive is apt to strip the gears.

   To engage the back gears (1st) Stop the lathe, (2nd) pull the Bull Gear Clamp Pin out of its engaging hole in the face gear so that the cone moves free on the spindle. (3rd) Then pull the back gear lever forward and re-start the motor.

6. While this running-in is going on you will have an opportunity to try the various controls on the apron, the reversing lever (Page 10), the change gears, etc. This time spent in "getting the feel" of your lathe and developing facility in handling it before starting work is time well spent. WARNING: Do not run the lathe at spindle speeds in excess of 500 R.P.M. during its first 10 hours of operation!

Care of the Lathe

A Sheldon lathe is a delicate precision tool with hand scraped ways and surfaces, any rust spot or battering of the ways, any chips or grit between close fitting parts is certain to affect the precise accuracy of this fine tool. For this reason:

• Whenever you finish working on your lathe wipe all *ways* and all machined surfaces with an oily rag— never leave your lathe without this thin film of protective oil over all parts that might rust.

• Never lay wrenches, cutting tools, files, etc. across the ways of your lathe as the slightest dent or burr on the ways will impair the accuracy of the lathe.

• Before inserting collars, centers or adapters or draw bar attachments in either spindle or tailstock spindle wipe each part in turn with a clean oily rag, and also wipe out all internal surfaces carefully with an oily rag on some type of improvised ramrod. Any chip or dirt remaining on centers or in spindle nose cannot only scratch or mar surfaces but will also interfere with the accuracy of the alignment of the assembled parts.

• Where Draw Bar Collet attachment is used be sure to lubricate draw bar thrust bearings frequently.

• If after long hard use you want to take up spindle bearing, it is easily done by (1st) tightening down spindle bearing caps and (2nd) removing any end play by first removing the 2 cap screws holding end housing, remove the socket set screws in spindle gear (often called bull gear) and striking the gear toward the spindle nose and the spindle nose toward the gear with *right and left hands* simultaneously. (Same motion as when clapping hands). Be sure that you do not over tighten so that spindle binds. After play has been taken-up, re-tighten spindle gear set screws.

• Play in the cross slide or in the compound is removed by tightening two set screws found at the front end of the taper gibs which lie in their respective dovetails.

• **Safety First:** While a lathe is an exceedingly safe tool to operate it has a few points of danger. Here are a few simple safety rules: (1) Never try to shift belts by hand until the lathe is completely stopped. (2) Never operate the lathe without first rolling up sleeves or tying sleeves down at wrists. Open or frayed sleeves have been known to catch on lathe dogs or "wind-up" in other revolving parts causing serious accidents.

Setting up
Lathe Tools

After selecting the cutter insert it in the tool holder permitting the cutter bit to project from the tool holder only far enough to provide the necessary clearance for the cutting point. Remember the closer up the cutter is held the more rigid the cutting edge.

Positioning the Tool Holder in the Tool Post

Tool holders are held in the tool post between the rocker saddle and the tool post screw. To assure maximum rigidity the tool holder should not be extended too far beyond the end of the compound rest. "B" in Fig. 40 illustrates about the proper clearance for both cutter bit and a turning tool holder.

Height of Cutting Tool in Relation to Work

After inserting the cutter in a tool holder and positioning the tool holder in tool post adjust the height of the cutting edge in relation to the lathe center before tightening the tool post screw. This is done by rocking the tool holder and tool post saddle in the convex cradle in which the tool post saddle rests. (Dotted line on Fig. 40)

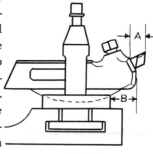

Fig. 40

48

Turning Tools

For all general turning operations set point of cutter bit slightly above the center line of the work. In steel the harder the material, the less above center. (Top, Fig. 41) Note the following exception, when machining soft brass, aluminum or materials that tend to "pull" or tear, set cutter on dead center. (Bottom Fig. 41)

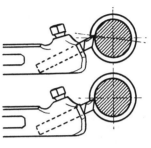

FIG. 41

On most turning and threading operations when cutting toward the headstock, the compound should be swung to hold the shank of the tool holder at an angle of approximately 20° to left of the perpendicular to the line of centers . . . EXCEPT when an extremely heavy rough forcing cut, working close to the limits, is being made. For such work, it is best to use a straight shanked tool held perpendicular to the line of lathe centers so that the tool will tend to swing out of the cut rather than "hog into" the work in case a stalling point is reached. (Fig. 43)

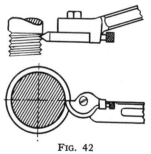

FIG. 42

Threading Tools

Threading tools should always engage the work on dead center as any deviation above or below the center will affect the profile of the thread. (Fig. 42)

49

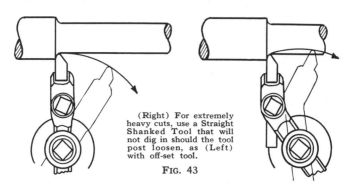

(Right) For extremely heavy cuts, use a Straight Shanked Tool that will not dig in should the tool post loosen, as (Left) with off-set tool.

FIG. 43

Cutting-off, Threading, Facing Tools

For cutting-off, thread cutting and facing operations the cutter should be fed to the work on dead center. (Fig. 44) For the beginner the average feed should not exceed .002 per revolution.

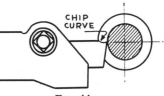

CHIP CURVE

FIG. 44

Boring and Inside Threading Tools

For Boring and Inside Threading the cutter point engages the work on dead center (Fig. 45) though the bar while parallel to the line of lathe centers can be positioned below center sufficiently to give the cutter

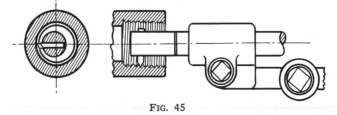

FIG. 45

a 14½° approach angle for greater cutting efficiency. On internal threading operations, you will note on grinding charts that follow, the top face of the cutter is ground to compensate for this angle, giving a flat "true form" top face.

Setting Up The Work
On Centers

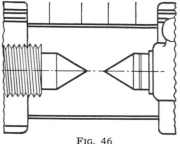

A shaft being turned down while being held between centers and rotated by a lathe dog and face plate. The tool in the tool post is a straight shanked turning tool holder.

Before setting up work on centers be sure Spindle Center and Tailstock Center are in accurate alignment. This is done by inserting center collar and center into spindle nose, and inserting Tailstock

FIG. 46

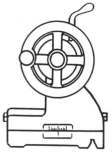

FIG. 47

Center into Tailstock ram, and moving tailstock up to headstock until the two centers touch. (Fig. 46) Any error in lateral alignment can be corrected by adjustment of Tailstock Set-over Screws. Be sure when aligned that set-over graduations are zeroed. (Fig. 47)

For most turning operations work is held in the lathe between the lathe centers by means of holes drilled in each end of the stock to be machined. The accuracy of the machining is primarily dependent upon the accuracy with which these are located at the center of the bar or block to be machined. The locating of this hole is called centering.

Centering is greatly facilitated where the ends of the work can be first squared so that you have a true cross section in which to locate the centering hole as explained later. But squaring or facing the ends in a chuck is the first lathe operation. This can be done with a file, but it affords excellent practice at facing in the lathe. First, chuck the stock in a 3-jaw universal chuck or, if your equipment does not include one, accurately centered in a 4-jaw independent chuck. Allow the stock to protrude about an inch from the chuck. Place a right hand Side Tool (or a straight turning tool with a "facing" cutter), (No. 9, page 25) in tool holder and clamp it in the tool post. Carefully adjust the cutting edge so that it is exactly on center. If this is not done a small "tilt" or projection will be left in the center of the stock which would later cause the center drill to run off center.

Start your lathe, using the slowest speed direct-cone drive and bring the tool into cutting position against the center of the work. Feed the tool *from the center of the stock outwards,* toward yourself, by using the hand cross-feed. One or two light cuts is usually enough to true up an end that has been roughened by the hack saw. After one end is faced, reverse the work in the chuck and face the opposite end.

Centering on long and round bars is done in several ways, with calipers, dividers or special centering instruments. (Fig. 48)

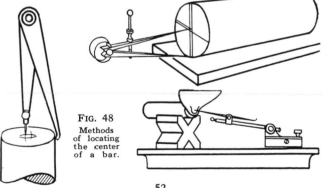

FIG. 48
Methods
of locating
the center
of a bar.

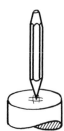

FIG. 50

Centering of square or rectangular stock in much the same manner. (Fig. 49) After center of each end is located a starting depression for for the drill is driven into the stock with a center punch. (Fig. 50)

FIG. 49

Checking Centers

After centers have been located with center punch, the accuracy of centers should be checked before drilling. This is done by placing work between the Spindle Center and Tailstock Center of the lathe and revolving

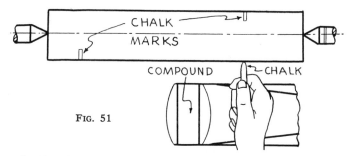

FIG. 51

the headstock slowly against a tip of the tool or a rigidly held chalk so that it just touches the high spots as illustrated in Fig. 51. If the center proves inaccurate (say .002 or more off) the position of the center should be corrected by re-punching at an angle.

Drilling and Countersinking Centers

After centers have been accurately located they must be drilled and countersunk to conform with the profile of the lathe centers so as to take the lathe centers without play or chatter.

FIG. 52

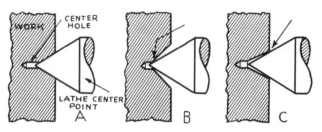

FIG. 53

Centers should be counterbored with a drill ground to a 60° point so that it will accurately fit lathe centers as "A". Too obtuse a counter bore ("B") or too acute an angle ("C") will give insufficient bearing, prevent accuracy, and will tend to destroy lathe centers.

This is best done with a combination Center Drill and Countersink, (Fig. 52) held in a tailstock Arbor Chuck. If a combination drill is not available centers can be drilled with a small drill and countersunk with any drill of sufficient diameter that has been ground to a 60 degree point—a 60 degree taper is standard for lathe center points. The depth of the center hole and countersink is determined by the heaviness of the cut to be made — the heavier the cut the deeper the countersink to provide sufficient bearing. Care should be exercised to get an accurate 60° countersink in center. (Fig. 53)

Mounting Work Between Centers

Remove chucks from the lathe, put the face plate on the spindle nose and put

FIG. 54

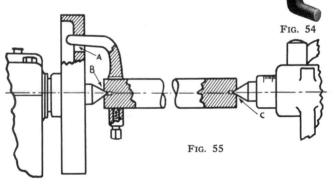

FIG. 55

both in headstock and tailstock centers. Fasten a lathe dog (Fig. 54) to one end of the work, put red lead mixed to a thick paste with machine oil in the opposite end which will ride on the tailstock or "dead" center and mount the work in the lathe as shown in Fig. 55. Before starting the lathe make sure that the work is not held so tightly between centers as to cause them to bind. Adjust the tailstock center so that the work turns freely and yet not so free as to allow end-play.

If after machining the work partially it is necessary to machine that part of the stock under the lathe dog, remove the work from the lathe and place the lathe dog on the machined end. Put red lead in the new tailstock center end and turn this end of the shaft down to the desired diameter or form.

NOTE: Before starting to machine work set up on centers, check carefully to see that the tail of the lathe dog is free in the face plate slot (does not tend to lift or pry stock off its true line of centers as in

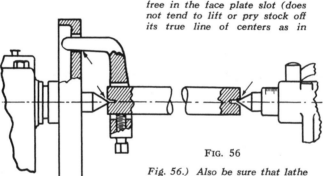

FIG. 56

Fig. 56.) Also be sure that lathe centers fit closely into center holes — sufficiently to eliminate all side play but still not tightly enough to bind. If working on a long piece be sure to check frequently to be sure that center is not binding as a result of expansion from heat generated by machining. Remember only the headstock center is live (revolves) the "dead" tailstock center serving only as a bearing upon which the work is revolved.

Use of the Clamp Dog

Standard Lathe dogs (Fig. 54) are designed to drive round or near round shapes. Rectangular or near rectangular stock requires the use of clamp dogs.

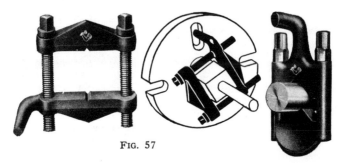

FIG. 57

In a properly made clamp dog the under face of the heads of tightening screws are convex and fit into concave seats, while the holes in the upper bar are not round but are elongated. This design permits considerable tilling of jaws from parallel and permits a firm grip of off-square shapes without bending of screws. Top and bottom bars should also have V-notches to permit a firm grip on triangular or other odd shaped stock. Clamp dogs, or special V-jaw dogs (Fig. 57 are also used for holding highly polished round bars.

Use of Faceplates in Setting-up Work

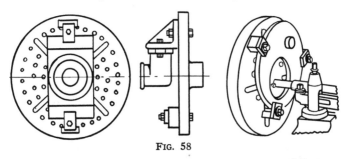

FIG. 58

In setting up work faceplates serve two different purposes (1st) to drive work held between centers and (2nd) to hold work of such shape that it cannot be chucked or mounted on centers. Faceplates used for driving work on centers are generally relatively small and are knotched and slotted to receive the tail of the lathe or clamp dog, bolt drive or other driving tool.

Faceplates used for holding work (irregularly shaped casting, machine or die parts, etc.) are usually larger than driving faceplates and of varied design—are T-slotted, drilled all over or slotted and drilled depending largely upon the work for which they are used. Work is mounted on such faceplates with T-slot Bolts, standard bolts, strap clamps, angle plates and other standard setting up tools. (Fig. 58)

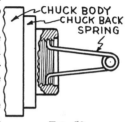

FIG. 59

As each job presents unique problems there are few general rules for setting up work on faceplates. However, two things are always important, namely: (1st) the internal thread of a faceplate should be cleaned to free it from dirt, chips or other matter that can interfere with its alignment or injure the spindle nose thread before screwing it on the spindle nose. This is easily done with a bit of spring wire formed as in Fig. 59. Unbalanced set-ups, as center illustration in Fig. 58, should be balanced with counter weight to overcome any "throw" as work revolves.

Setting-up Work on a Mandrel

Cylindrical or bored pipe work, or cored castings too long to be held in a chuck, are machined by being mounted first on a mandrel which in turn is mounted between centers. (Fig. 60) The solid mandrels which are driven into the hole of the work must of course, be tight enough to turn work against the tool without slippage, and should be lightly oiled before being driven into the work. Otherwise, work is apt to freeze to the mandrel making it impossible to remove the mandrel after work is completed without injury to both work and mandrel.

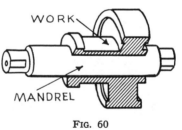

FIG. 60

When removing a mandrel be sure to drive it back out of, instead of on thru the hole—drive it out in an opposite direction than you drove it in.

Hardened steel mandrels can be purchased which have a slight (.003 in.) ground taper and an expanding collar to facilitate mounting and de-mounting work (Fig. 61). Mandrels are also available with compres-

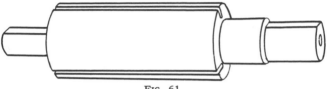

FIG. 61

sible ends for holding single or ganged pieces. Once mounted on a mandrel work is machined in the same manner as a solid shaft. Eccentric centers can be drilled in mandrel ends to permit eccentric turning on a mandrel.

FIG. 62

Use of Steady Rests and Follower Rests

Rests are used for (1) setting up work that is relatively long in proportion to diameter, or (2) work on which the dead end must be left free for boring or other operations, and (3) for machining slender shafts which are apt to spring out of alignment from the thrust of the tool. The purpose of a rest is to support the work and maintain it in accurate alignment so that it may be accurately machined. Rests though differing in design are basically classed as "Steady Rests" or "Follower Rests".

The Steady Rest

A Steady Rest mounts on the bed of the lathe, is clamped over the ways and provides 3 bearing surfaces that bear lightly but rigidly against the surface of the shaft and prevent its movement out of the line of lathe centers. A steady rest can be placed at any point along the lathe bed where it will best support and steady the work without interfering with the operation being performed. (Fig. 62)

To set up a steady rest (1) center work in chuck and true up. (2) Slip the steady rest into position and tighten it to the bed. (3) With bearing jaw clearing work, close the top of the rest (if of standard hinge type) and tighten locking screw. (4) With lathe running adjust the 3 bearing jaws to touch but not push the work. (5) Test again for alignment to be sure that the axis of the work coincides with the axis of the lathe —otherwise the end will not be square and surfaces and boring will be untrue.

The Follower Rest

Long shafts or slender shafts that are apt to be sprung out of alignment by the thrust of the cutting tool often require the use of a follower rest. (Fig. 63)

FIG. 63

A follower rest mounts on the carriage of the lathe and hence moves with the tool, backing up the work opposite the point of tool thrust. Follower rests have 2 adjustable supporting jaws; one holding the work down to prevent the tendency to climb up on the tool, the other is behind the work to counter the thrust of the tool.

> *NOTE: Great care should be taken in adjustment of jaws of rests as they must form a true axial bearing for the work, must allow the work to turn freely but without play.*

Setting-up Work in a Chuck

Work that is too short to be conveniently held between centers and work requiring machining at, into (as boring or inside threading) or across its end is usually held in a chuck. While it is possible to set-up such work on a faceplate with special setting-up tools or even as in olden times, tying it to a faceplate, the convenience of chucks have made them part of every complete lathe. Lathe chucks come in sizes that will hold work of diameters approaching the swing of the lathe and are of many types, including automatic and high speed air operated production chucks. For ordinary use, headstock chucks are of two standard types: 1st) The 4-jaw Independent Lathe Chuck which because its four holding jaws can be operated independently of each other, can be adjusted to hold round, square, eccentric or odd shaped work. (Fig. 64) (2nd) The 3-jaw Universal Geared Scroll Chuck which holds

FIG. 64

FIG. 65

only round or near-round work with 3, 6, 9, 12 or other "multiple" numbers of sides and always holds work concentrically has the advantage of being self-centering—all jaws moving in or out together. (Fig. 65)

If a lathe is to have but one chuck, it should be a 4-jaw Independent Chuck because it is the most universal. If the lathe is to be fitted to two chucks, the second should be a 3-jaw Universal Gear Scroll Chuck because on the types of work it handles chucking time is greatly reduced by its self-centering feature.

THE SIZES OF CHUCKS FOR SHELDON LATHES

Lathe Swing	4-Jaw Independent Lathe Chuck		3-Jaw Self-Centering Gear Scroll Chuck	
	Recommended	Maximum	Recommended	Maximum
10 inch	6-inch	6-inch	5-inch	5-inch
11 inch	6-inch	8-inch	6-inch	8-inch
12 inch	8-inch	10-inch	8-inch	10-inch

FIG. 65

Chucks are manufactured so that they can be mounted on any size or standard make lathe. They are mounted by means of a Chuck Plate. (Fig. 65) Chuck plates are provided by each lathe manufacturer threaded to accurately fit the spindle nose thread of the particular lathe, and semi-machined to fit standardized machined recesses found in the back of every standard chuck. The fitting of a chuck to chuck plate and the squaring of a chuck to the spindle nose while not difficult or complicated must be done with extreme accuracy. For this reason it is recommended that it be done by the lathe manufacturer wherever practical.

Mounting Work in a 4-Jaw Independent Lathe Chuck

For small diameter, short work jaws should be inserted in the chuck with high ends to the center to give maximum gripping and maximum tool clearance (Fig. 66). For large diameter work on the other hand, jaws are inserted in chuck slots with the high steps of the jaws to the outside of the chuck (Fig. 67).

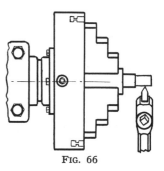

FIG. 66

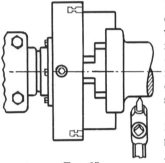

1. **To place work in chuck:** Adjust chuck jaws to approximate opening to receive the work roughly centering them by matching nearest concentric ring on chuck face with corresponding mark on jaws. (Fig. 64)

2. Place work in chuck and grip it turning up opposing jaws a uniform number of turns with key provided, sufficiently to hold work in position. Then bring in the other pair of opposing jaws in the same manner.

FIG. 67

3. Revolve the spindle slowly with left hand while holding a piece of chalk so that it just touches the high point (the nearest surface) of the work. (Fig. 51, page 53)

4. Guided by chalk marks re-adjust jaws until a chalk line will carry completely around the work. Then tighten all jaws securely. When making several identical pieces after finishing work release only two adjoining jaws leaving the other to hold the center. Jaws of 4-jaw independent chucks are reversible—can be inserted with high steps inside or to the outside. (Figs. 66, 67 and 68)

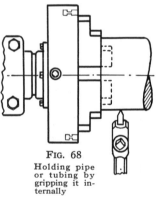

FIG. 68

Holding pipe or tubing by gripping it internally

WARNING—*Never leave the chuck key (wrench) in the chuck while the chuck is on the spindle, as any movement of spindle can crash it into ways causing serious damage to the ways, spindle and chuck. Remembering that each jaw of a chuck whether "Independent" or "Universal" type has stamped on it a number which corresponds to a number stamped on the chuck near one of the slots. Always put a jaw in the slot with its corresponding number, because EACH JAW FITS ONLY ITS OWN SLOT! Never remove a chuck or heavy face plate without first laying a board across the ways to protect the ways in case the chuck drops slightly when it comes off the spindle nose.*

Mounting Work in a 3-Jaw Universal Geared Scroll Chuck

Work in set up in a 3-jaw Universal Scroll Chuck (Fig. 65) in the same manner as in the 4-jaw independent chuck with these exceptions: (1st) On these chucks the key moves all jaws at once. (2nd) There is no "centering" or checking of concentricity as these chucks are automatically self-centering. (3rd) Jaws are not reversable—each chuck coming with two sets of jaws—one set of jaws for set ups with high steps toward the inside and the other set for mounting in the chuck with the high step to the outside.

Standardization of Lathe Spindle Threads

As a further effort toward standardization in machine tools, a movement is under way to get lathe manufacturers to co-operate in adopting uniform threads for lathe spindles so that chucks will not have to be fitted individually to each lathe. With the general adoption of some such standardized spindle thread and other standardized means of mounting lathe chucks, chucks will be interchangeable from one lathe to another. Four standardized types of chuck mountings as now proposed by chuck manufacturers are illustrated below.

American Standard Type A-1   Cam Lock Type D-1

Long Taper Key Drive Type E   Threaded Spindle Noses

Other Types of Chucks Used on a Lathe

Other smaller chucks are provided for special use on a lathe, among them: (1) Spindle Nose Chucks, (2) Tailstock Chucks and (3) a Center Rest Chuck. The first two are of the self-centering 3-jaw key operated type commonly used on drill presses, portable drills, etc. The Jacobs, key operated, Spindle Nose Chuck is a small 3-jaw universal chuck which fits onto the spindle nose thread and is used to hold drills, reamers and small work. It functions as both a small capacity 3-jaw chuck, in that it is self-centering; and as a universal collet, in that it has a hollow center, will hold small work, and permits the feeding of stock thru the spindle. While a spindle nose chuck has the advantages of being a universal tool for it will hold a range of sizes (i.e. $\frac{1}{8}$" to $\frac{5}{8}$" or $\frac{1}{4}$" to $\frac{3}{4}$" etc.) and is fast in operation it can-

Spindle Nose Chuck

Tailstock Chuck

Center Rest Chuck

not equal a precision made collet in accuracy, operating speed or holding power. Some spindle nose chucks (those for large size lathes) often do not mount directly on the lathe spindle nose but on a hollow taper arbor which replaces the live center. (Fig. 69)

The Tailstock Chuck, as its name implies, mounts on a tapered arbor that replaces the dead center in the tailstock. It is used for drilling, center drilling, reaming etc. as described later in this book.

The Center Rest Chuck also mounts on the tailstock. It has concave jaws and serves as a rest rather than as a chuck, is used to support (externally like a center rest) the dead end of

Fig. 69

64

small diameter shafts that cannot be drilled for a center such as centerless armatures, etc.

Collets and Collet Attachments

For holding small diameter work, whether bar stock fed thru the hole in the spindle or small bits or pieces as semi-finished parts, a collet attachment is preferable to standard chucks: (1st) because collets have a much faster releasing and gripping action; (2nd) because they automatically and *accurately* center the work; (3rd) because they will take a firm grip on even small pieces and where only a short hold is possible, and (4th) because, being housed within the spindle nose, a collet gives maximum tool clearance—makes it possible to machine, thread or cut-off close up to the very spindle itself. While chucks are universal tools that will hold stock of a range of sizes and shapes, collets are special tools— an individual collet being provided for each size and for each shape to be held. (Fig. 70 and Fig. 71)

FIG. 70

Round Square Hexagonal

Made with extreme accuracy,

Cut-away drawing of Slotted Collet

FIG. 71

hardened and ground, the standard split collets are slotted to permit the compressing of their jaw ends inwardly to grip the work to be held. The Collet Jaws are compressed by pulling the externally tapered shoul-

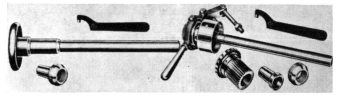

FIG. 73   FIG. 72

der of the collet jaw into a matching taper-bored Sleeve. This is done by means of a Hand Wheel Draw-in Collet Attachment (Fig. 73), or a Hand Lever Draw-in Collet Attachment. (Fig. 72)

The Hand Wheel type draw-in collet attachment consists of (1) A hollow bar with a hand wheel on the left end which goes thru the hole in the lathe spindle. (2) A flanged sleeve with a tapered hole bored in the end which inserts into the spindle nose, the flange of which covers and protects the end of the spindle. (3) A threaded collar which goes over the spindle nose thread, and (4) one or more split collets. (Fig. 74)

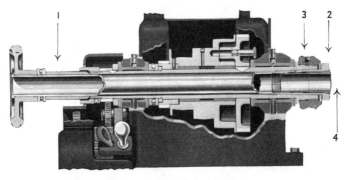

FIG. 74

The collet end of the draw bar is internally threaded to receive the threaded end of the collets. By turning the hand wheel the collet is drawn into or pushed out of the Taper Bored Sleeve. By thus pulling the externally tapered jaws of the collet into the internally tapered sleeve the collet is compressed or permitted to spring open, gripping or releasing the work to be held. (Fig. 72) Hand Wheel Draw-in Collet Attachments are widely used in tool rooms for making and holding small parts. In high speed production work Lever operated Draw-in Collet Attachments (Fig. 73) are more frequently used because of their greater operating speed. In operation they work in the same manner but collets are drawn in by lever rather than turning up a screw thread.

Tool Post Grinders

Every fully equipped lathe should have a tool post grinder . . . a small independently operated grinding head complete with integral electric motor that is designed to mount as a unit in the tool post T-slot of the compound rest. (For lighter work some are held in the tool post.) So mounted, it can be maneuvered in the same manner as any cutting tool. Tool post grinders come with wheels of different shapes, sizes and grits for grinding different materials and surfaces, and with arbors and mounted wheels for grinding internal surfaces. They are used where surfaces must be "ground" or polished — for grinding lathe centers, arbors, taper sockets, leader pins, gauges and valve seats and other close fitting parts, as well as for sharpening milling cutters and similar tools.

Setting-Up a Tool Post Grinder

Before placing a Tool Post Grinder on the compound, carefully wipe T-slot and the base of the grinder free from all grit and chips. For most grinding operations the wheel must engage the work at dead center in the horizontal plane of the lathe centers. Align the center of the grinder spindle vertically with the tailstock center (an elevating screw is provided for this purpose), and clamp it securely when aligned. Next accurately adjust the angle of the compound rest. The grinder is fed to the work with the compound rest feed and any single cut or "pass" should not exceed .001 inch.

WARNING: Before using a tool post grinder always cover the lathe bed, especially the ways and the cross feed with paper or oil cloth to prevent the abrasive dust from the grind wheel getting into any working parts or on hand scraped surfaces. On finishing work remove the tool post grinder and carefully wipe off lathe bed, carriage, compound, tool post T-slot etc., with an oily rag to make sure that all grinding dust has been removed. Any negligence in this can destroy the accuracy of your lathe.

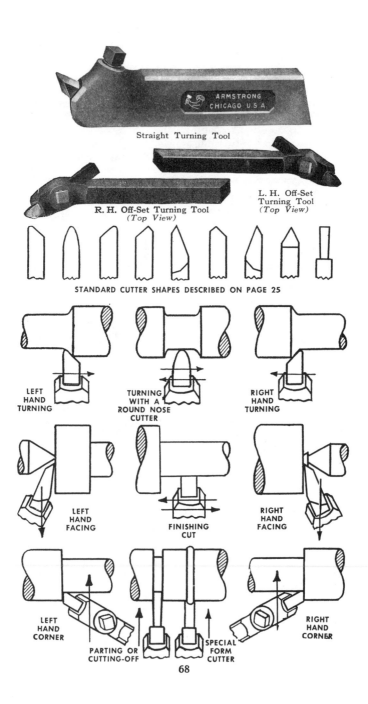

Straight Turning Tool

R. H. Off-Set Turning Tool
(Top View)

L. H. Off-Set
Turning Tool
(Top View)

STANDARD CUTTER SHAPES DESCRIBED ON PAGE 25

LEFT
HAND
TURNING

TURNING
WITH A
ROUND NOSE
CUTTER

RIGHT
HAND
TURNING

LEFT
HAND
FACING

FINISHING
CUT

RIGHT
HAND
FACING

LEFT
HAND
CORNER

PARTING OR
CUTTING-OFF

SPECIAL
FORM
CUTTER

RIGHT
HAND
CORNER

68

ROUGH TURNING . . . A heavy cut with a straight shank tool holder.

Turning

Rough Turning

In turning a shaft to size and shape when there is a great deal of stock to be cut away, heavy, rough cuts are taken in order to get the work done in the shortest possible time. Heavy cuts should be made with the transverse power feed; from right to left—toward the headstock so that thrust is against the live center. For this cut the cutter should be a "Right Hand" Turning or "Round Nose" Cutter. (Page 68)

The cutter should be held in a Straight Shanked or L. H. Offset Turning Tool. The L. H. Offset Turning Tool is theoretically more rigid for heavy cuts because it lies with its shank parallel to the center line of the compound when the compound is off-set to the right approximately 20 degrees. In such position both Compound and Tool Holder Shank are more nearly in line with the direction of maximum thrust. (Page 49) *Though the L. H. Offset Turning Tool Holder has the advantage of theoretically greater rigidity, it is safer for the novice especially, to use a Straight Shanked* Turning Tool Holder held perpendicularly to the line of centers, when making extremely heavy cuts so that if there is any loosening of the tool post the tool will swing away from, rather than into the finished work. (Fig. 43, page 50) The point of the cutter engaging the work is just above or on the line of centers. (The greater the diameter of the work the higher the cutter can be placed above center) (Fig. 41) The height of the cutter is easily adjusted by rocking the tool holder on the saddle of the tool post. With your tool so positioned, tighten the tool post screw. Run the carriage to the right end of the work with the hand wheel on the apron. Be sure the Power Feed Lever on apron is in the (left hand) position of quadrant to engage the longitudinal feed; and that the lathe is set to feed toward the headstock (Reversing Lever is at top position). Then start the lathe. Run the cross feed in by hand to take as heavy a cut as is consistent with the power of your drive or the amount of metal to be removed and engage the longitudinal feed by turning in the clutch hand nut. In every case be sure to take a cut of sufficient depth to reach below the scale on oxidized bars or iron castings otherwise the hard oxidized surface will dull the tool rapidly.

Finish Turning

When the work has been rough turned to approximate finished size (within 1/32") replace your "rough" cutter bit with a freshly ground keen edge cutter and make one or more light finishing cuts across the machined surfaces. Check diameters carefully with caliper or micrometer to be sure that you are working to proper dimensions. Remember the diameter will reduce twice the thickness of the cut.

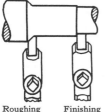

Roughing   Finishing
FIG. 75

While most mechanics prefer a deep cut and a comparatively fine feed for *rough* turning, the reverse is true for *finishing cuts* which are usually made with a very light cross feed and coarse transverse feed with a cutting edge that is wider than the feed per revolution. In Fig. 75 the left hand tool diagramatically illustrates the first roughing cut and the right hand tool the following finishing cut.

Turning to Shapes

Other turning cuts, machining shapes, corners, fillets, etc., are performed in the same manner, differing primarily in the selection of cutter bits and the maneuvering of the cutting point by means of the various feeding controls on the apron. As illustrated on page 24 a single modern tool holder with a few cutters any mechanic can grind from stock shapes of high speed steel will do the work of a complete set of old style forged tools. Application of standard tools for turning operations are are also illustrated on page 68.

Machining Square Corners

To machine an accurate corner (1) Set compound perpendicular to line of centers, insert corner tool (R.H. or L.H.) (2) Using longitudinal feed, turn small diameter to finish size up to shoulder (3) Then using compound rest feed tool, amount needed to finish work to length taking last facing cut across shoulder away from the center. (Page 68)

Finishing and Polishing

After machining where a very smooth polished surface entirely free from machine marks is desired it can be obtained best with a tool post grinder. If a tool post grinder is not available tool marks can be removed with a file by taking full biting strokes across the revolving work at a slightly oblique angle. Do not drag the file back across the work, lift it clear for each return stroke. Use a clean dry file and see that work, too, is clean. Wipe work dry and clean if a coolant or cutting oil has been used. Never hold the file stationary while work is revolved. (Fig. 76)

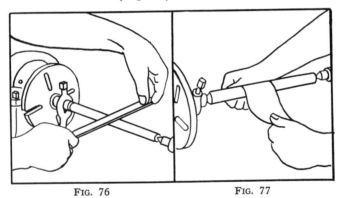

FIG. 76   FIG. 77

After machining marks have been removed with a file, work may be polished with an emery or other abrasive cloth. Lathe should be turning a high speed and a few drops of oil should be spread along the work. is desired it can be obtained best with a tool post grind- The cloth should be kept moving along the work. (Fig. 77)

Taper Turning

There are three ways to turn a taper on an engine lathe (1st) with the compound rest (2nd) by setting-over the tailstock and (3rd) with a Taper Attachment. In all methods the cutter must engage the work on dead center if the taper is to be accurate. Tapers cut with the compound usually are short, abrupt angles, such as centers, bevel gear blanks and die parts. (Fig. 78)

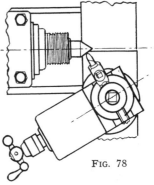

FIG. 78

These are generally not considered under the classification of "taper turning" which more specifically applies to the machining of longer more gradual tapers.

While it is possible to turn long and gradual tapers without a Taper Attachment by setting-over the tailstock of the lathe, this method is in many ways unsatisfactory both mechanically and practically because to do so requires considerable mathematical computation involving many factors, error in any one of which will spoil the work. It also requires changes of position of centers and of tailstock which is almost certain to affect the accuracy of centers if other machining operations follow on the same shaft. It also throws counter-

FIG. 79

sunk centers in ends of shaft out of alignment with the lathe centers and greatly reduces their bearing surface. ("A"-"A" Fig. 79)

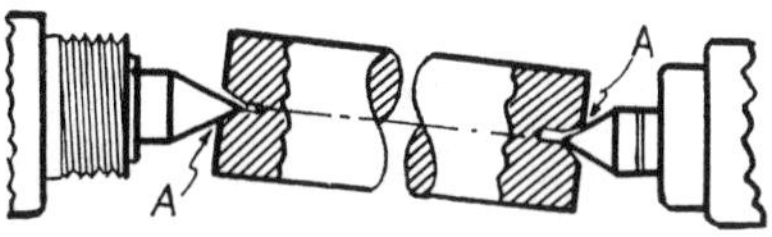

Turning a Taper without a Taper Attachment

Where a lathe is not equipped with a taper attachment, the taper is cut by setting over the lathe tailstock so as to give a disalignment of lathe centers,

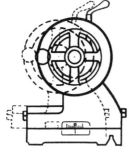

FIG. 80

from their parallel with the transverse travel of the tool, sufficient to give the desired degree of taper. (Fig. 80) The tailstock of Sheldon lathes have a set-over scale calibrated both forward and backward from the straight turning or zeroing point for measuring the distance of set over. On lathes with no set-over scale the set-over can be measured as in Fig. 81.

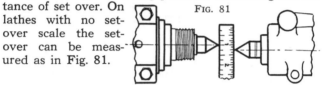

FIG. 81

Determining the Correct Set-over

The distance of tailstock set-over required to machine any given taper is dependent upon four factors, namely: (1) The differential between the finished diameters of the extreme ends of the taper. (2) The length of the taper in relation to its extreme diameters if the entire shaft is to be tapered. (3) The ratio between length of tapered portion, to the entire length of the shaft (or work between centers) being machined when only part of the shaft is to be tapered.

Where the taper extends the entire length of the work the tailstock set-over should be equal to ½ the differential between the finished diameters of the ends.

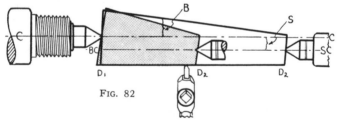

FIG. 82

NOTE: A given set-over does not give a fixed degree of taper because the shorter the shaft the greater will be the degree of taper resulting. Fig. 82

Where the taper extends but a portion of the length of the shaft to be machined. To find the correct set-off for the tailstock, divide the total length of the shaft by the length of the portion to be tapered and multiply the resulting quotient by ½ the difference between the extreme diameters of the finished taper.

> NOTE: *Most drawings give the taper in inches-per-foot of length and are sometimes more easily computed by conversion of all dimensions to inches.*

> NOTE: *Be sure to zero the tailstock before resuming straight turning.*

Boring a Tapered Hole

Without a Taper Attachment this is done by setting the compound at the desired degree of taper and feeding the tool with the compound. *Remember when setting up for this operation that the compound is set at ½ the degree of angle of the completed taper hole.*

Turning Tapers with Taper Attachments

Sheldon taper attachments are of two types: Plain Taper Attachments and Telescopic Taper Attachments. Either type greatly simplifies the turning of tapers and

(Above) Sheldon Telescopic Taper Attachment
(Below) Sheldon Plain Taper Attachment

boring tapered holes and the cutting of external or internal threads on tapered surfaces. Both permit greater degrees of taper than can be obtained by setting of the tailstock. Permanently attached to a lathe they in no way interfere with straight turning or other operations when not in use. A taper attachment permits the machining of tapers of any length and the following with other operations (straight turning, threading, etc.) on the same shaft without change of set-up or loss of centers; permits the machining of duplicate tapers even on stock of varied lengths and the turning of tapered shafts and identically matched taper bored holes from the same set up.

Both types (Plain and Telescopic) consist of (Fig. 83): (1) backward extension of the cross slide that is bolted on machined pads that are ready-tapped to receive it. (2) A supporting bracket which is bolted to the back of the carriage saddle. (3) A compound slide of which the top swivels and has calibrations on the

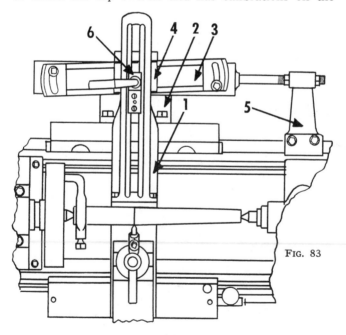

FIG. 83

right end to indicate angularity in inches per foot and other calibrations on left end of swivel which indicates angularity in degrees. (4) A sliding shoe that moves transversely along swivel slide and is attached to the extension of the lathe cross slide. (5) A clamp bracket which locks the taper attachment at any position along the lathe bed when in use, and which when taper attachment is not in use slides free along the lathe bed with the movement of the lathe carriage. (6) Is a locking nut or handle which locks the cross stud extension, 1, to the sliding sleeve, 4, at the point which will bring the tool to the correct position (determined by the diameter of the work). Standard industrial taper attachments permit the cutting of tapers to 8½ inches in length with a single setting and of any length with multiple settings.

Operating a Plain Taper Attachment

To operate a Plain Taper Attachment it is necessary to first disengage the Cross Feed Screw so that the compound rest can slide free on the cross slide and hence be guided by the taper attachment. So, (1st) disconnecting the nut thru which the screw cross feed travels, (2nd) move the carriage and Taper Attachment to the part of the lathe bed where taper is to be cut, (3rd) position the swivel slide so that it will allow the carriage to travel along the length to be tapered and tighten the set screw (or screws) of the clamp bracket (to the lathe bed). (4th) Set the top of the swivel taper guide at the proper angle (to give the degree of the taper desired). This is easily done with the aid of one of the scales on the end of the swivel guide, one of which is graduated in inches of taper-per-foot, the other in degrees of taper. This type of calibration eliminates need for mathematical computation as tapers are usually given in "taper per foot" or in degrees, which, if no degree scale is given on your type taper attachment are readily converted to inches-per-foot by reference to any hand book or taper table. (5th) Set the compound at 90° with the line of the finished taper. Turn the compound feed back all the way and move the cross slide to a position at which the tool point will just clear the "high" corner or point to be machined and tighten the sliding shoe lock nut.

Starting on the high corner proceed as in any straight turning operation adjusting the feed of the tool for successive cuts with the compound rest feed screw. (This is your only means of advancing the tool to the work as the cross feed is disengaged.) As the carriage moves along the bed the sliding shoe of the Taper Attachment travels with it holding the tool in a line parallel to the angle at which the swivel slide of the taper attachment has been set.

Operating a Telescopic Taper Attachment

Telescopic Taper Attachments are identical to Plain Taper Attachments except that they have the improvement of a telescopic cross feed screw *which does not have to be disengaged for taper turning.* This feature not only obviates the need for disconnecting and reconnecting the cross feed screw nut, it also permits the normal cross feed control of the tool and simplifies greatly the transition from straight to taper turning, and from taper turning back to straight turning.

> *NOTE: Tool Holder must be set up (1st) Perpendicular to the normal (not set-over) line of centers of the lathe, and (2nd) so that cutter point is exactly on dead center. Any variation above or below the dead center will result in work that is not truly conical as the rate of taper will vary with each succeeding cut. Fig. 84.*

> ● *After re-engaging cross feed screw (not necessary with telescopic taper attachment) be sure to loosen set screw that locks taper attachment Clamp to lathe bed and set screw that locks Cross Slide Extension to Sliding Shoe of Taper Attachment before resuming straight turning or other machining operations.*

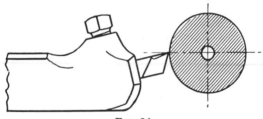

FIG. 84

Facing

Before removing work from centers the ends should be faced—that is, squared up. In fact, on accurate work especially where shoulders, bevels, etc. are to be at accurate distance from ends, the ends are usually faced before the shank is turned—not only to clean and square up ends and to give a finished end from which to make calibrations but also to machine the work to accurate length.

Especially where diameters are large facing is best done with a special "side" tool holder which holds a long thin blade with a wide cutting edge. (Fig. 85) However, where no side tool is provided it can be done with a long narrow pointed cutter well extended from a

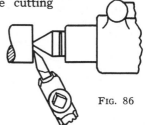

FIG. 86

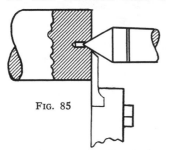

FIG. 85

turning tool holder, (to assure clearance between work and center). The *tool should be fed from the center outward* in order to avoid marring the lathe center. (Fig. 86)

Facing Across the Chuck

When facing (cutting across) stub end work held in the headstock chuck the same rules apply except that, cutting edge must be set on the exact line of center so that there will be no remaining tit at the center. While a "side" tool is preferable for this type of work because of its smooth slicing cut it can be done with an ordinary turning tool, or better an off-set turning tool because no clearance problems are present such as we have between centers at the ends of a shaft. When facing with a turning tool be sure to cut from center to outside. Do not start with a heavy feed because the feet-per-minute cut increases rapidly as the cutter moves thru ever increasing peripheries. This requires "reverse" grinding of bit. (an R. H. Offset Tool Holder would take an L. H. Cutter).

FACING across the chuck with an L. H. Off-Set Side Tool.

Knurling

Knurling is not strictly a machining operation as no metal is cut. It is rather a forming operation in that hard patterned knurls are pressed into work, depressing and raising the surface of the metal into the knurl

Diamond Pattern, Standard Face Straight Line Pattern, Full Face

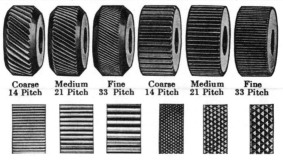

| Coarse 14 Pitch | Medium 21 Pitch | Fine 33 Pitch | Coarse 14 Pitch | Medium 21 Pitch | Fine 33 Pitch |

Above Knurls. *Below* Pattern each makes.

KNURLING—Note tool angle and self-centering
feature that equalizes the pressure on the Knurls.

pattern. As with all other forming operations, the work
can be no better than the pattern—your knurling no
better than your knurls. Be sure that knurls are sharp
and clean-cut (preferably hob-cut) and properly hardened. Since to make a true uniform knurling the pressure on both knurls must be uniform, select a knurling
tool that is self-centering, that automatically equalizes
the pressure on the knurls and has sufficient strength
to withstand the terrific end and side thrusts encount-
ered in this operation.

Before starting to knurl, remove the work from the
lathe and scribe lines indicating the part to be knurled.
In knurling, the back gears must be used and the lathe
operated at slowest back-geared speed for best results.
Always engage the back gears while the lathe is idle
(never when it is running as this can strip
the gears).

Knurling exerts extreme thrust against
centers and bearings. This thrust can be
materially lessened if the knurling tool is
fed to the work at a slight angle off from
perpendicular to the line of the work, so
that the right side of the knurl engages
the work first. (Fig. 87)

FIG.
87

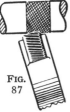

81

Place a few drops of oil on the part to be knurled and on the knurling tool. Start the rolls (knurls) of the knurling tool from the right-hand scribe line and feed them in until the knurl reaches a depth of 1/64 in. After knurling for a small fraction of an inch, stop the lathe and inspect the work. If the knurl is not clear cut, adjust the tool in or out until it is. Now use plenty of oil to keep both knurls and work covered. Then start the lathe and engage the automatic feed so as to move the knurls across the portion to be knurled. When the left scribe line is reached, force the tool into the work another 1/64 in. reverse the lathe without removing the tool and feed back to the starting point. The feeding both ways should be done by using the automatic longitudinal feed. Once across, each way, usually makes a good knurl.

Cutting Screw Threads

SCREW THREAD CUTTING TOOL

Since screw thread cutting is so generally a part of machine work, anyone interested in building things of metal should master this phase of mechanics thoroughly. It is not difficult. Rather, it requires a bit of patience and skill that comes only from practice. Before attempting to cut a thread on anything actually being made in the shop, the novice is advised to cut a few practice threads on odd bits of steel and iron. Then there will be little danger of spoiling a piece of work that is partly done.

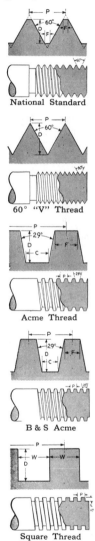

National Standard

60° "V" Thread

Acme Thread

B & S Acme

Square Thread

Sheldon lathes are built for screw cutting and will cut all standard internal and external threads as well as innumerable special screw threads. Threads may be cut "coarse" or "fine" (in a great range of numbers of threads per inch), "V" or square shapes, worm threads or in the established profiles such as American National Standard, Acme, or Whitworth. Threads can be cut either right-hand or left-hand; either single threads or in multiple threads that run concurrently along the shaft. The type of thread to be cut is determined by the use to which the screw is to be put. Each form of thread requires a differently shaped tool with which to cut or "chase" it.

For the most work, however, the beginner will usually use either American National Coarse Thread (formerly U. S. Standard) or American National Fine Thread (formerly S. A. E. Standard). Both of these are "V" form threads, slightly flat on top and at the root of the thread. Screw threads are usually referred to by "pitch" numbers, such as 18 or 24, etc., meaning 18 and 24 threads per inch respectively. All Sheldon lathes will cut all standard threads in all pitches from 4 to 112 per inch.

The experienced worker can compound the gears forming part of the lathe's equipment according to well established rules and thus cut any number of different pitch threads he desires. The Sheldon lathes which are equipped with a quick-change gear box, eliminate the need for the extra "pick-off"

Whitworth Thread
(British)

gears and gear changing as all gears are permanently in the gear box and are changed mechanically by movement of the gear box lever. Since compounding cannot be done by hand on the quick-change gear lathe, an extraordinarily large number of different threads are provided for on the index plates of this type of lathe. (Fig. 90)

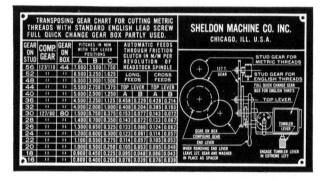

TRANSPOSING GEAR CHART FOR CUTTING METRIC THREADS WITH STANDARD ENGLISH LEAD SCREW FULL QUICK CHANGE GEAR BOX PARTLY USED.										SHELDON MACHINE CO. INC. CHICAGO, ILL. U.S.A.
GEAR ON STUD	COMP. GEAR	GEAR ON BOX	PITCHES IN M/M WITH TOP LEVER POSITIONS			AUTOMATIC FEEDS THROUGH FRICTION CLUTCH IN M/M PER REVOLUTION OF HEADSTOCK SPINDLE				
			A	B	C					
56	127/110	44	7.000	3.500	1.750					
52	''	''	6.500	3.250	1.625	LONG. FEEDS		CROSS FEEDS		
48	''	''	6.000	3.000	1.500					
44	''	''	5.500	2.750	1.375	TOP LEVER		TOP LEVER		
40	''	''	5.000	2.500	1.250	A	B	A	B	
36	''	''	4.500	2.250	1.125	0.458	0.229	0.428	0.214	
32	''	''	4.000	2.000	1.000	0.408	0.204	0.385	0.193	
30	127/80	80	1.500	0.750	0.375	0.153	0.077	0.143	0.072	
28	''	''	1.400	0.700	0.350	0.143	0.072	0.133	0.067	
26	''	''	1.300	0.650	0.325	0.133	0.066	0.124	0.062	
24	''	''	1.200	0.600	0.300	0.123	0.061	0.114	0.057	
22	''	''	1.100	0.550	0.275	0.114	0.057	0.105	0.053	
20	''	''	1.000	0.500	0.250	0.105	0.053	0.095	0.048	
18	''	''	0.900	0.450	0.225	0.095	0.048	0.086	0.043	
16	''	''	0.800	0.400	0.200	0.076	0.039	0.076	0.039	

(Diagram text: STUD GEAR FOR METRIC THREADS; STUD GEAR FOR ENGLISH THREADS; FULL QUICK CHANGE GEAR BOX FOR ENGLISH THR'DS; 127.T. GEAR; TOP LEVER; TUMBLER LEVER; GEAR ON BOX COMPOUND GEAR; END LEVER; WHEN REMOVING END LEVER LEAVE 32T. GEAR AND WASHER IN PLACE AS SPACER; ENGAGE TUMBLER LEVER IN EXTREME LEFT)

However, since the Sheldon "Metalworker" comes without a quick-change gear box and Sheldon lathes can be had with semi-quick, change gear (rather than full quick change gears) boxes and require the use of auxiliary pick-off gears to obtain all possible thread-cutting combinations, a brief explanation of the mechanical workings of a lathe in thread cutting will be of interest to those desirous of knowing the "how and why". Since the lathe spindle (which carries the work) is connected by gearing, to the lead screw (which moves the cutting tool along the lathe bed) a definite ratio exists between the speed of the spindle in revolutions per minute and the movement of the cutting tool in inches. (Fig. 4, Page 8)

When you change the gearing you change this ratio. For this reason you can cut screw threads of various pitches merely by changing the pick-off gears at the head end of the lathe or the set of the gear box lever.

The rules for calculating gear ratios to cut special threads is a simple one as shown below:

A—number of threads per inch on lead screw

B—number of teeth in spindle gear, called stud gear

C—number of threads to be cut (per inch)

D—number of teeth in screw gear

Formula:

$$D = \frac{B \times C}{A}$$

For example you wish to cut a 24 thread and the lead screw thread is 8 per inch. Look into your stack of gears and select a small one. Count its teeth and select it as your first choice for (B), the spindle gear, (or stud gear). Supposing it to have 16 teeth; then your formula would give you

$$D = \frac{16 \times 24}{8} = 48.$$

Or more plainly, $16 \times 24 = 384$. Dividing this product by (A), the lead screw pitch of 8 threads per inch, the result is 48. You would then need a 48-tooth gear for the screw gear. If you do not have a 48-tooth gear select another small gear from the change gear stack for the spindle gear and try again; for example you select a 20 tooth gear.

$$D = \frac{20 \times 24}{8} = 60.$$

You would in this case put the 20 tooth gear on the spindle and the 60 tooth gear on the lead screw.

Lathes are sometimes equipped with compound gears such as 2 to 1, ratios, etc. In the above example if you use a 20 tooth gear on the spindle you can use a 2 to 1 reduction compound gear on the screw, and secure the same results.

Most threads are right-hand threads, hence the threading or chasing tool is started at the right-hand end of the work and is fed towards the headstock. In cutting a left-hand thread, the direction of rotation of the lead screw and reverse gears are reversed and the threading tool is fed from left to right.

While with practice it is possible to grind cutters to almost any profile, it is difficult to sharpen such cutters without altering the cutting form and every re-sharpening usually requires a complete regrinding of profile and clearance angles. For that reason it has become almost universal practice to use threading tool holders that take special form cutters that require only flat, top grinding to re-sharpen (Fig. 91) and hence always maintain their true profile. Such form cutters are available for all standard threads. For the novice especially, the use of such threading tools is the best guarantee of true profile, accurately fitting threads.

FIG. 91

Threading Form Cutter that requires only flat top grinding (along line "A"-"A") to resharpen. After grinding cutter should be rotated to horizontal position for use.

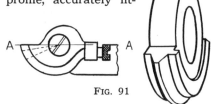

FIG. 91

Thread and Thread-cutting Terms

The rapid development of industrial activity led to such confusion of thread designs, numerous "standards" definition terms that in 1928 the Congress of the United States authorized a National Screw Thread Commission to establish a standard system for screw threads. This lead to the American National Screw Thread System

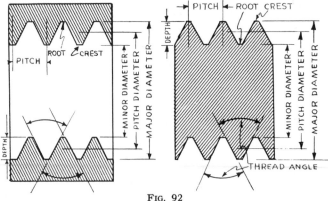

FIG. 92

and a uniformity in terminology. The principle new standard terms are illustrated in Fig. 92 and following paragraphs.

On drawings and instructions made before 1928 the *Major Diameter* was often referred to as the "outside diameter" or "full diameter". The *Minor Diameter* was formerly called the "cored diameter" an "inside diameter" etc.

The Pitch has always referred to the distance from any given point on a thread to the corresponding point on the next thread.

The Pitch Diameter (used more in engineering than in machining) is the diameter of an imaginary cylinder superimposed on a straight screw thread, the surface of which would make equal the width of the thread and the width of the spaces cut by the cylinder.

The Lead is the distance a screw thread advances axially (as thru a nut) with one complete revolution. The lead and pitch of a single thread would be identical but would be different on multiple threads, i.e. the lead of a double thread would be twice its pitch, if a triple thread, three times its pitch, etc.

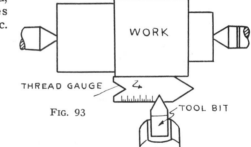

Fig. 93

Cutting a Screw Thread

After turning the work to be threaded to the "major diameter" of the thread and setting gears for the thread desired, set-up a threading tool in the tool post, and set it *exactly on dead center* of the work to be threaded, using a thread gauge to guide you as in **Fig. 93**. Place the thread gauge on the point of the threading tool and feed the tool toward the work. The tool should be adjusted so that the edge of the gauge is exactly parallel to the work. A slip of white paper held below the gauge will help to check the parallel of gauge to shaft and the fit of the tool point in the "V" of the gauge. Threading tools have an off-set head or means of adjustment which permits the holding of the cutter perpendicular to the surface of the work (thereby assuring a true-form thread), while the shank of the tool holder and the compound rest are approximately perpendicular to the primary cutting edge of the cutter, the right hand 60° side of the cutter form. (Fig. 42)

With the tool properly positioned turn the dial of the thread chasing dial to the correct "zero" (as explained on page 91) and engage the thread chasing dial gear. Then clamp the half nuts of the lathe on the lead screw, after placing the automatic feed knob in neutral position. Take the extra precautions of making sure that the lathe dog is securely fastened to the piece to be threaded as the slightest slippage will ruin the thread; also that the tail of the dog does not "bottom" on the face plate slot. (Fig. 56) Have oil or red lead on the tail center where it enters the work.

The adjustable thread-cutting stop should be used in thread cutting. It is possible to cut an accurate thread without it, but difficult. Its purpose is to limit the travel of the threading tool within the fixed limits of the Major Diameter and Minor Diameter of the thread being cut. The Sheldon Thread Cutting Stop (Fig. 94) remains on the lathe and is engaged or disengaged by the swinging stop hook on the carriage over the stop rod. This type has stop points for

Fig. 94

both major and minor depths and after completing a thread can be disengaged (unhooked), other machining operations performed and the set still held for duplicate screws or matching nuts. But to get back to our thread cutting:

Bring the point of the tool up to the work. Adjust the extention of the stop (to compensate for variance in diameter of the work) and lock the stop rod with the socket set screw "S". Fig. 95

Swing the hook up from the carriage and over the stop rod. Then tighten knurled thumb next "A" up against the hook. Then set the thumb nut "B" to a position which will make the distance between "A" and "B" equal to the depth of the thread to be cut. When ready to take the first chip, run the tool rest back slightly by using the cross feed screw, then turn screw "A" one-quarter turn to the left. This will allow the point of the tool to take about 1/64 in. on the first chip. Before taking each cut thereafter, turn the adjusting screw of the thread cutting stop ¼ turn to the left until nut "A" is backed up tight against nut "B", advance slightly and take a light chip each time across the thread.

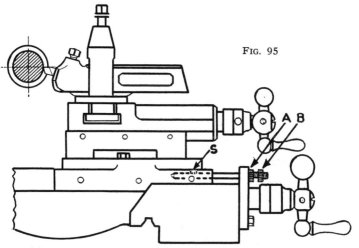

Fig. 95

To actually take the first chip, move the point of the tool about ⅛ in. away from the surface of the metal. Move the carriage so as to bring the point of the tool a little to the right of the end of the work, clamp the half-nuts firmly on the lead screw and start the lathe, using slowest back-geared speed and keeping plenty of oil on the tool point and on the work. This can be done with a small paint brush if lathe is not provided with a coolant pump. Feed the tool to the work as far as the thread cutting stop will allow and take the first chip.

When the tool reaches the end of the cut, withdraw it by turning the cross feed screw to the left at least one complete turn so that the tool will clear the thread on the reverse travel of the carriage. If using a countershaft driven lathe, reverse the direction of the feed of the carriage by reversing the shipper rod; if using a motor driven lathe, reverse the motor. This reverses the direction of the feed of the carriage which travels back automatically. Do not disengage the half nut from the lead screw at any time until the thread is finished.

When the point of the tool reaches the starting point, stop the lathe and measure the thread to see if you

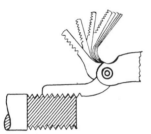

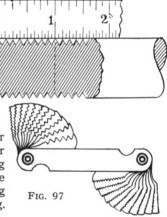

have the correct pitch (or number of threads per inch) either by counting thread against a steel rule (Fig. 96) or by applying a screw Pitch Gauge (Fig. 97). Adjust the thread cutting stop by unscrewing ¼ turn and take the second chip, following the same operation as before, and continue until the thread is finished.

FIG. 97

Using a Thread Dial Indicator

All Sheldon lathes except the "Metalworker" come equipped with a Thread Chasing Dial. (Fig. 98) attached to the lathe carriage and actuated directly by the lead screw the thread chasing dial indicates accu-

Fig. 98

rately the point at which to re-engage the double half-nuts on the lead screw for successive cuts. With a thread chasing dial it is not necessary to return the tool to the starting point of the cut by reversing the motor and waiting for the tool to return all the way thru the cut to the starting point. With a Thread Chasing Dial the operator can at the finish of each cut disengage the split nut and return the carriage to the starting point quickly with the hand wheel because the Thread Chasing Dial shows the exact point at which to re-engage the double half-nuts to bring the tool accurately into the groove for the next cut.

Rules for Operating the Sheldon Thread Chasing Dial

The face of the Sheldon Thread Chasing Dial is graduated and numbered into divisions. This dial is revolved by the lead screw so that each graduation passes a zeroing point on the stationary part of the dial housing.

When cutting even threads, (an even number per inch) the half-nuts can be engaged at the point at which any graduation aligns with the "zero" mark. When odd threads (an odd number of threads per inch) the half nuts can be re-engaged as any *numbered* graduation aligns with the "zero" mark.

When cutting *half threads* (such as 4½, 5½, 11½ etc. threads per inch) the half-nuts can be re-engaged as any *odd* (1, 3, 5) number graduation aligns with the "zero" mark.

Don'ts for Thread Cutting

A few don'ts for thread cutting might include: don't remove the lathe dog until the thread has been finished and tested; don't disturb the spindle while the work is off the centers. When you think the thread is about finished and ready for testing, remove the work from centers, leaving the dog attached. Test the thread in the threaded hole of the tail jaw you are making. If the thread does not fit properly and needs another chip

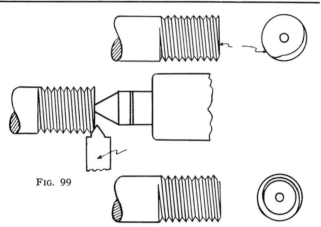

FIG. 99

or two, place the work back in the centers exactly as it was before, take the required chips and test again. Repeat until finished.

Finishing-off a Threaded End

After cutting a thread and before the threading tool is removed the end should be finished by being chamfered as shown in Fig. 99. This not only improves the appearance but removes all sharp corners and burrs but also will aid the screw in engaging a nut or threaded hole.

Cutting Left Hand Threads

Left hand threads are cut in identically the same manner as right hand threads except that the carriage feed is toward the tailstock instead of away from it, cutter clearances should be reversed, the cutters must be ground back with clearance angle on the left side, and the compound rest should be swung to the left rather than to the right.

Multiple Threads

Multiple threads are cut one at a time in identical manner to single threads except that lead is increased to make room for succeeding threads (a double lead for a double thread, a triple lead for a triple thread, etc.). After the first thread is completed the work is removed from centers *without loosening the lathe dog* and is then replaced in the lathe with the tail of the lathe

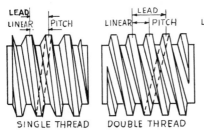

SINGLE THREAD   DOUBLE THREAD   TRIPLE THREAD

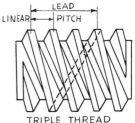

LEFT HAND THREAD

dog in the correct slot to index the work for the next thread. This work requires a face plate with accurately positioned slots uniformly spaced and equal in number to the number of threads to be cut.

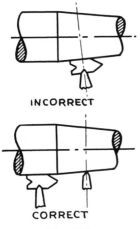

INCORRECT

CORRECT

Fig. 100

Cutting a Thread on a Taper

Thread cutting on a taper is performed in the same manner as on a straight shaft except in the setting-up of the tool. Either without or with a taper attachment the threading tool is set at 90° to the *axis* of the taper rather than at 90° to its surface. (Fig. 100)

93

Drilling and Boring

Drilling on a lathe can be handled in two ways—with the drill held stationary and the work revolved, or, with the work held stationary and the drill revolved. Drilling with the drill held stationary in a tail stock chuck is the more accurate method (gives a straighter hole) and is also the most frequent method because without change of set-up (and re-centering) work is ready for any succeeding operations such as boring and internal threading.

In all lathe drilling keep the drill sharp and properly ground. This is essential to get a straight accurate sized hole (Charts for proper drill grinding are obtainable from drill manufacturers). With high speed steel drills, operating speeds are not so critical but where carbon steel drills are used high speeds can quickly "burn" a drill. The number-of-feet-per-minute rule applies to drills even more rigidly than to other cutting edges (because there is practically no opportunity for air cooling of the point after it has entered the hole). The larger the drill the greater the number of peripheral feet cut per revolution — hence the slower should be the drilling speed. Where no drilling speed data is available one is generally safe to run drills under ¼ inch diameter up to 750 R.P.M., drills up to ½ inch at 500 R.P.M. and larger drills at proportionately slower speeds.

Fig. 101

With work held to headstock and drill in tailstock chuck the drill is fed into the work by advancing the tailstock ram. This is done by turning the tailstock hand wheel. (Fig. 101) It is always advisable to have a locating center for the drill point, made with a center punch or even a countersunk center for large diameters to prevent the drill from creeping. When no tailstock chuck is available or is of too small capacity, drill can be held in a Drill Holder. Drill Holders are of two types: for holding taper shank drills (Fig. 104), and for holding straight shanked drills (Fig. 105).

When drilling in a long shaft or work that extends a distance from the headstock chuck, it is necessary to provide another point of support for the work in order to overcome the tendency set up by the torque of the drill to twist work sideways. This support is provided with either a Center Rest or Follower Rest. (Page 58)

Drilling with a "Live" Drill on the Lathe

When it is necessary to drill work which cannot be chucked in the lathe it can be done by reversing the drilling method described above by chucking the drill in the headstock end and using a Crotch Center or

95

Drill Pad in the tailstock to serve as a table or base for holding the stock. These useful accessories have a tapered stem and fit into the tailstock ram in place of

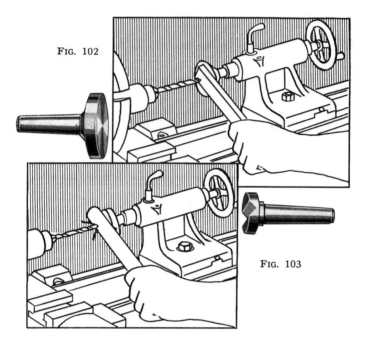

FIG. 102

FIG. 103

the tailstock center. The Crotch Center automatically centers round work for cross drilling or for holding irregular shapes much as a V-block does on a drill press. The Drill Pad provides a flat base for drilling flat stock or drilling holes that are not to be centered.

For such drilling drill is held in a spindle nose chuck and the stock is held in the left hand against the drill pad or crotch center and is advanced to the drill by turning the tailstock hand wheel with the right hand. (Fig. 102-Fig. 103) Since the torque of the drill tends to force the stock against the bed of the lathe when drilling large work in this manner, it is well to place a block of wood across the bed to protect the hand scraped V-ways against marring by the stock.

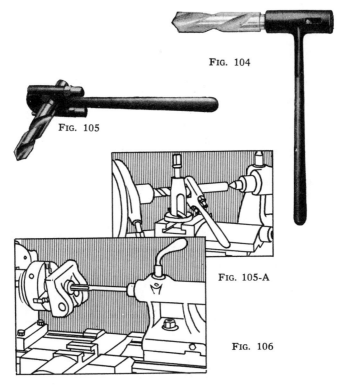

FIG. 104

FIG. 105

FIG. 105-A

FIG. 106

Reaming

When a hole must be accurate to within .002 inch or less, it should be first drilled slightly underside (.010 to 1/64 in. on small diameters and from 1/64 to 1/32 on hole of from 1 to 2 in. diameter) and then reamed either by hand or in the lathe. Lathe reaming is usually done with solid reamers either held in a tailstock chuck or with a taper shank that fits the tailstock ram in place of the tailstock center. (Fig. 106) When reaming on a lathe use slow speeds and feed the reamer into the work slowly and evenly. Be sure that reamer teeth are free from burrs and chips.

Boring

Boring is internal turning — turning from within. Because in much work the diameter of the opening to be bored is much less than its depth, boring tools must be of relatively small diameter and still be capable of supporting a cutting edge projected at considerable distance from the tool post or compound rest. All boring tools by their nature consist of an extremely stiff and strong bar with either a formed cutting end or means of holding a high speed steel cutter. There are many sizes and types of boring bars all consisting of a bar or several interchangeable bars and some means of holding it. In selecting a boring tool be sure to get the one that will give the stiffest possible bar at every depth and diameter and the greatest choice of cutters and cutter angles. (The ARMSTRONG 3-Bar Boring Tool illustrated on page 94 is of the multiple bar type).

Note that boring bar is extended from holder only far enough to give clearance.

This light boring tool holder has wide gib to overcome tendency to chatter.

It is also desirable to select tools with smooth ended
bars, without projecting each nut or other hardened
edges which might mar the work. (Fig. 107) Modern

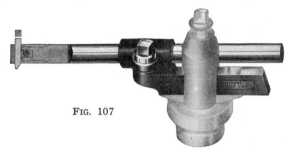

boring tools take cutters of standard high speed steel
shapes which usually have but one cutting edge, though
double end cutters offer advantages in special instances.
(Fig. 110) In grinding cutters allow sufficient end rake
to provide clearance from internal diameter (see grinding charts pages 30-32).

Except when boring cored casting, pipe or tubing the
boring operation starts with a drilled hole of sufficient
size to admit the end of the boring bar. Since the holes
in cored castings often tend to deflect or spring a boring bar off center or from its true axis, it often is ex-
pedient to chamfer or turn out a starting cut in the
opening of the hole to be bored with turning tool, before introducing the boring tool. (Fig. 108) With
boring tool holder set up (in tool post or tool post "T"
slot depending on type) select the largest diameter
boring bar which with cut-
ter will be acceptable by
the bore. Extend the bar
from the holder only far
enough to reach the full
depth to be machined and
still allow tool clearance.
Except where the "adjust-
able" boring tool is used
(for extremely large di-
ameter work) the bar is

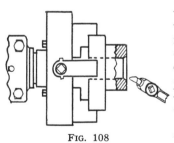

Fig. 108

99

fed into the hole to be bored parallel to the axis of the hole. The cutting edge of the cutter engages the work along a line in the mounted plane of the lathe centers with the bar in a position that gives the cutter a top rake of approximately 14° from the radius at the cutting point —this takes into consideration the ground angle (top rake) of the cutter itself. (Fig. 109) For straight longitudinal cuts, the cutter can be held close-up, hence more rigidly, if held at an angle of 90° to the bar. However, for machining ends of bar it is necessary to have a boring bar that will hold cutter at an angle or angles which will permit the extension of the cutter beyond the end of the bar. (Fig. 110) It is generally most convenient to position the cutting edge at the near side parallel to the center line as this position gives maximum visability of the work being done.

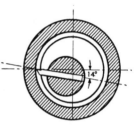

FIG. 109

The general rules that apply to external turning, apply to boring except as noted in cutter grinding instructions where rake angles differ — are governed by manner of holding cutter and diameter of bore; and feeds are necessarily lighter to prevent springing the tool. This is espe-

FIG. 110

cially true when enlarging an out-of-round hole, take several small cuts rather than one heavy cut. After the last finish cut it is common practice to reverse the feed and take a last fine cut with tool coming out of the work. This cut is taken without movement of the cross feed and avoids a slightly undersize hole by compensating for any "spring" in the bar.

Cutting Internal Threads

The rules controlling internal thread cutting are much the same as for external thread cutting except that in internal thread cutting the same clearance re-

strictions and tool problems are
present as in boring operations.
The same tool holders are used
for internal thread cutting that
are used for boring except that
cutters have thread forms and
are fed at thread cutting ratios
of feed to spindle revolutions.
(See pages 81-92) Another difference between boring and inside threading is in the cutting
angle at which the cutter ap-
proaches the work. As with
external thread cutting, the internal threading tool must engage the work on dead center
and must be held so that the
cutter coincides with the center
radius of the work. (Fig. 111)

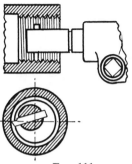

FIG. 111

In squaring the cutter with
the work a center gauge (Fig.
112) or thread gauge should be
used to correct any error in the
alignment of cutter. Internal
cutter requires greater end and
side clearance and length of cut-

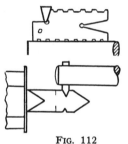

FIG. 112

ters is also restricted as internal thread cutters must
have enough end clearance to permit the cutter to be
lifted clear of the thread for removal. (Fig. 111, Top)
Before cutting an internal thread the work is first bored
to the exact major diameter. (Fig. 92)

Remember the feed of successive cuts is toward (instead of away from) the operator and the set of the
thread cutting stop is therefore reversed. Secondly, due
to the extension of the cutter from the tool post, cuts
must be lighter. An extra finishing cut should be taken
without changing the setting of compound rest.

Cutting Special Form Internal Threads

Internal forms are cut in all of the thread forms used for external threads. There is only one factor that calls for special attention in cutting internal threads of special shapes and that is the difference of clearances be-

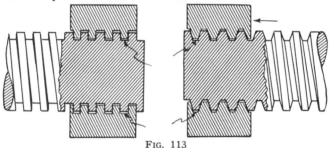

FIG. 113

tween nut and screw recommended for the different thread types. (Fig. 113) Where these special recommended clearances are not available it is a safe rule to cut a nut (internal) thread from .005 to .010 in. per inch larger in major diameter of the screw.

Cutting Off or Parting

Cutting off in a lathe is done only when one end of

FIG. 114
Cutting-off with an R. H. Off-Set Spring Cutting-Off Tool.

the work is rigidly held (as in a chuck) and is not practical for long work between centers not closely supported with a rest nor where free section is long enough to sag and pinch the blade. It requires a "tight" lathe without any excess play in spindle, compound, carriage or the tool post because any play or looseness is almost certain to cause chatter. It requires a narrow cutting edge with ample side clearance (from 5° to 10°) (Page 25) which should be fed into the work slowly to prevent "hogging-in". Once considered a difficult and costly operation cutting-off has been made much simpler by the development of special narrow cutting-off tool holders with special cutting-off blades. (Fig. 114) Of these new cutting-off tool holders the spring type is recommended especially for cutting-off tough alloy steel, soft metals, cored casting, tubing and similar work where hard spots (or a break thru in tubing) tends to cause the tool to "hog-in". The goose-neck form of the "spring" type cutting-off tool not only eliminates chatter but also allows the blade to "duck" hard spots and prevents the work from climbing up on the blade—the cause of most cutting-off tool breakage.

A cutting-off tool should be held in the tool post as close-up as possible, with the blade on dead center and exactly perpendicular to line of centers. The blade should be extended only far enough to pass thru the  work just beyond its center. (Fig. 44) The tool should be fed to the work, on exact center, *slowly and evenly* with the cross feed. If the tool "hogs-in" and stops spindle rotation, stop the motor and reverse the spindle by hand before backing the tool out with the cross feed. Always set up work to cut off as close to the headstock as possible. If it is necessary to make a "parting-cut" on a long shaft or on work between centers never complete the cut in the lathe, finish the parting with a hack saw and return it to the lathe for facing. Spindle speeds should be slowed down until a "feel" for cutting-off has been developed and though lubrication or coolants are not essential on small diameter work they should be amply supplied on deep cutting-off work.

INDEX

INDEX (Continued)

INDEX *(Continued)*

PRINTED BY
GENTRY PRINTING CO.
CHICAGO

ROSS LLEWELLYN, INC.
CHICAGO   U. S. A.